Authors Series

Bowman, *Editor*

ANA UNIVERSITY

ANN RADCLIFFE

by E. B. Murray

The list of superlatives unarguably attached to Ann Radcliffe's name belie the relative obscurity in which she purposely enwrapped her private life and which posterity has accorded her since her death 150 years ago. She was the greatest, the most significant, perhaps the best, and (with the exception of Horace Walpole) the first of the Gothic novelists. In her day she achieved a popular acclaim which none of her great predecessors among English novelists—Richardson, Fielding, Sterne, and Smollett—had approached. And the critics of the time generally aligned themselves with this popular consensus. As a transitional figure between an Age of Reason and an Age of Romanticism, she influenced giants among early nineteenth-century English literature such as Coleridge, Byron, and Shelley. Jane Austen wrote an affectionate satire on her works, the Brontë sisters converted her villains into their heroes, and even the sentimental realism of Dickens here and there shows strong evidence of a Radcliffean Gothic influence. The success of her works provided the incentive behind the flood of Gothic novels which inundated the English reading public during the 1790's; Matthew Lewis's *The Monk,* Mary Shelley's *Frankenstein,* Charles Maturin's *Melmoth the Wanderer* stem more or less directly from *The Mysteries of Udolpho* or other Radcliffean terror epics; the twentieth-century resurrection of the Gothic, from Bram Stoker's *Dracula* to the cinema werewolf, testify to the continuing popular vitality of this sub-genre sprung almost full grown from the head of this demure, decorous, and rather pretty product of a dying rationalism and an embryonic romanticism.

The modern reader and student is likely to ask what was there about Mrs. Radcliffe's works which justified her immense popular and critical acclaim

Ann Radcliffe

(TEAS) 149

Ann Radcliffe

By E. B. MURRAY

University of Missouri-St. Louis

and her later and continuing influence on writers greater than herself. Here is a detailed account of the intriguing development of a minor talent finding her way to near-greatness through an increasingly intense and thoroughly romantic involvement with her own terrific and awe-inspiring creations. Here is a skeleton key to Radcliffean Gothic in whatever century (including the present) it may be found.

ABOUT THE AUTHOR

Professor E. B. Murray did his undergraduate work at Kenyon, his graduate work through the Ph.D. at Columbia. He has taught at Rutgers, Indiana University, and is presently an Associate Professor of English at the University of Missouri-St. Louis. His area of special study is English Romantic literature; he has published several articles and major scholarly reviews in learned journals here and abroad on important Romantic writers including the poets Keats and Shelley.

To Pierrette

Preface

My purpose in this book has been to find out precisely what went into the composition of Mrs. Radcliffe's novels. In trying to achieve that purpose I have attempted a detailed analysis of certain portions of those novels that seem best to illustrate both the form and the content of her art. In order to eliminate as much redundancy as possible when discussing novels which tend to repeat each other not only in form and content but also in characterization, I have often allowed what I say, for example, about the heroine's "sensibility" in one book to stand as a commentary applicable to the others as well, unless something new has been added in a given novel. I have included portions of Mrs. Radcliffe's accounts of her travels in England and on the Continent which evidence striking parallels between her reactions to scenery and Gothic decor when she saw it and when she imagined it for her novels.

In a general summary of the historical background of Radcliffean Gothic I have included generous excerpts from usually unread and barely extant novels of the last quarter of the eighteenth century. I hope these excerpts will help condition the reader to an appreciation of the moral and esthetic tradition justifying the decorous swoons and tremblings of a Radcliffean heroine. My feeling is that the reader needs to confront that tradition not merely in paraphrased generalizations about it but in the very words and exclamation marks which passed current from novel to novel as the appropriate expressions of a hero or heroine whose sensibility is forever on the stretch.

I have tried to trace Mrs. Radcliffe's increasingly complex use of these sentimental conventions from the two-dimensional fast-action of *The Castles of Athlin and Dunbayne* through the structural counterpointing of *The Mysteries of Udolpho* to the intensely dramatic confrontations of *The Italian*. Partly because of the crudely disjointed exposition and simple anatomy of *Castles*, this first novel lends itself to some discussion of the primary virtue of the Radcliffean (and conventional) heroine—disinterestedness— which is, in a rudimentary way, set off ethically and esthetically from the calculated self-interest of the villain. *The Sicilian Romance* develops the villain's complexity, the sentimental heroine replaces the medieval hero and his trappings as the center of interest, and the ghostly effects which had been minimal in *Castles* exit finally into a characteristic Radcliffean *"expliqué."* *The Romance of the Forest*, Mrs. Radcliffe's first major novel, suggests the structural use of decor as a means of heightening terror and suspense by its nearly microcosmic use of the heroine's room as a not very solacing retreat from the real horrors of the outside world to the inner horrors of the parasupernatural. In the *The Mysteries of Udolpho*, La Vallée, Udolpho itself, and finally the Villefort château, serve to base and test the heroine's sentimental education, and seem to indicate a moral as well as an esthetic purpose behind the larger structural divisions of the novel. *The Italian* makes the reader's imagination a stage on which the dramatic vignettes of *The Romance of the Forest* are intensified and concentrated in the several diabolical dialogues and confrontations which develop the mixed character of Mrs. Radcliffe's one superlative creation, Schedoni. In developing the kind of emphasis from novel to novel that I suggest here, I have generally avoided the descriptive vocabulary associated with the terrific sublime on the grounds that most commentators have used it almost to the exclusion of any real analysis of what occurs in Ann Radcliffe's books.

I have dealt only with the five Gothic novels. The posthumously published *Gaston de Blondeville*, in spite of its real ghost (or partly because of it), is not part of Radcliffean Gothic. Mrs. Radcliffe's poetry, while occasionally transcending mediocrity, is neither important nor relevant. I have used the Ballantyne text almost exclusively simply because it is the least inaccessible text which contains all of the novels I deal with. I have at times modernized the punctuation where it appeared a needless obstacle in the way of understanding a passage.

Finally, I would like to thank the University of Missouri-St. Louis for the grant and leave-of-absence which facilitated the completion of this study.

Contents

Preface

Chronology

1. Life and Times   13
2. The Gothic Background   29
3. *The Castles of Athlin and Dunbayne*   61
4. *The Sicilian Romance*   75
5. *The Romance of the Forest*   90
6. *The Mysteries of Udolpho*   112
7. *The Italian*   135
8. Evaluation and Influence   159

Notes and References   169

Selected Bibliography   173

Index   175

Chronology

1764   July 9, Ann Ward born in London.
1787   Married William Radcliffe.
1789   *The Castles of Athlin and Dunbayne.*
1790   *A Sicilian Romance.* 2 vols.
1791   *A Romance of the Forest. Interspersed with some Pieces of Poetry.* 3 vols.
1794   *The Mysteries of Udolpho. A Romance. Interspersed with Some Pieces of Poetry.* 4 vols.
1795   *A Journey made in the Summer of 1794 through Holland and the Western Frontiers of Germany.*
1797   *The Italian, or the Confessional of the Black Penitents.* 3 vols.
1815   *The Poems of Ann Radcliffe.*
1823   February 7, died.
1826   "On the Supernatural in Poetry, "*New Monthly Magazine,* vol. 7. *Gaston de Blondeville, or the Court of Henry III keeping Festival in Ardenne. A Romance; St. Alban's Abbey. A Metrical Tale.*

CHAPTER 1

Life and Times

IN 1764, medieval chivalry, Romantic enthusiasm, and sheer sensationalism were combined in classic form with the publication of the first Gothic novel, Horace Walpole's *The Castle of Otranto*. On July 9 of the same year, Ann Radcliffe, the "mighty magician" destined to refine and transmute the spectacular crudities of Walpole's thriller into an appropriate form for "sensibility," the sublime, and the picturesque, was born in London, the only child of William and Ann Ward. Walpole's well-documented public career contrasts with the ascertainable facts of Ann Ward Radcliffe's secluded private life quite as much as the Gothic extravagances of Walpole's *Otranto* contrast with the suggestive obscurities of Mrs. Radcliffe's *The Mysteries of Udolpho*.

Radcliffean Gothic is essentially a development of the eighteenth-century novel of sensibility along the lines suggested by Walpole when he joined the sentimental commonplace of parental tyranny with a chivalric ghost story. However, Mrs. Radcliffe's tableaux do not drip with blood, like Walpole's, but with psychological tension. Whereas Walpolean Gothic is steeped in breathlessly disconnected fast-action, shock on shock, vintage Radcliffe wiredraws a single incident through page after page of premeditated suspense. Unlike Walpole, Mrs. Radcliffe was not satisfied with dreaming her way out of an oppressively routine society through a sort of rudimentary and uncalculated surrealism. There is no evidence in her representative novels of giant bodies growing piecemeal out of the woodwork or falling indiscriminately from outer space. She was willing to tinker with, but not ignore, rational limits of the eighteenth-century empirical psychology her readers were morally and esthetically conditioned to accept. Neither she nor her readers could take any vital interest in a bit of fourth-dimensional adventuring in a world otherwise quite two-dimensional.

A prime reason why Walpole's Gothic innovation had no emulators to speak of during the quarter-century that passed between its publication and Mrs. Radcliffe's first works is that it lacked even a conventional moral depth. And it lacked moral depth because its supernatural phenomena had no metaphysical or psychological motivation more sophisticated than the sort of superstition Mrs. Radcliffe lets only her maidservants—never her heroines—believe in. For her, Gothic terrors had in some way to be moral tests for her heroine, which they could never be if they remained irrational and whimsical. Mrs. Radcliffe clearly luxuriates in the moral dilemmas of her heroines—they are quite as titillating to her and should be to her readers as the decorously modified terrors she took over from Walpole, or the sublime landscapes she took over from the paintings of Salvator Rosa and made part of her Gothic art.

There are certain conventional props of the Gothic novel which have not much changed from Walpole through Radcliffe to the present-day variants on their themes. Battered castles, abbeys, subterranean passages, flickering candles, bats, rusty locks, creaking doors, dungeons, skulls, blood-encrusted daggers, darkness, dankness, and mold are the perennial delights of anyone who has it in him to delight in the Gothic novel. Mrs. Radcliffe's distinctively subdued use of the conventional trappings stemmed from her esthetic and probably moral decision to keep her readers in a state of animated suspense rather than in a state of insensible shock. Walpolean Gothic or its variants were based in the incredible, the irrational, the superstitious, and the utterly fanciful. Radcliffean Gothic was explainable at last—it was rational, spiritual, and imaginative, if only in quite conventional ways.

The surrealism which Walpole suggested in his dream-fantasy required an imaginative sophistication which had to be built up in the reading public before it could be appealed to in any serious way. Without knowing it, Mrs. Radcliffe bridged part of the gap Walpole unwittingly had tried to leap over by offering an eclectic, superficial, transient but perfectible literary synthesis of a moribund rational morality and an emergent Romantic esthetic. A twentieth-century writer states the problem and the challenge a twentieth-century reader faces when trying to accommodate his esthetic responses to the values of an outmoded convention:

This cocoon of clichés and ready-made ideas, which we never stop producing, covers everything, even to the most authentic works of art. It even conceals from us the great literary works of the past . . . to grasp their living always new reality, we are obliged to extricate them from the envelope of conventional handed-down concepts that covers them, divest them of what is most apparent, often too most worn, most obsolete, most facile: that is, imagery that has become banalized, out-of-date sentiments, characters whose aliveness is that of wax dummies, rudimentary psychology, a plot that satisfies the reader's curiosity and excitement at the same time that it leads him away from pure esthetic joy. If we consider the greatest literary works, how many readers had they, or have they today, who in order to appreciate them, are capable of making such an effort as this? [1]

I *Facts and Anecdotes*

Coincidence seekers may gather some solace from the fact that the "Shakespeare of romance" was not only born exactly two hundred years after her namesake but also, like him, left little besides her works to record her life. In a "Memoir" prefixed to Mrs. Radcliffe's posthumously published *Gaston de Blondeville*,[2] T. N. Talfourd dignifies his subject and pads the sparse detail of her life by advising us that, while her father was in trade (he was a haberdasher), her relatives were of independent fortune. At the residence of one of these, an uncle mentioned as a friend of Josiah Wedgwood, she could have met certain minor literary lights of the day. When her family moved to Bath in 1772, she was at least in a position to attend the school for young ladies later opened there by Sophia Lee. It is likewise reasonable to suppose that the publication of Miss Lee's sentimental historical novel *The Recess* (1785) impressed Ann Ward with its Gothic overtones; and it might have paved the way for her own initial attempt at historical Gothic four years later in *The Castles of Athlin and Dunbayne* (1789).

Somewhere, Ann Ward received the young-ladylike education of her day—a bit of the Classics, some literature, perhaps some language, certainly some music and some drawing—the kind of education she later provided for her heroines. There is no question that she knew portions of Shakespeare's tragedies quite well; her favorite German work, we are told, was Johann Schiller's *The Robbers*—but that Gothic thriller was not available to her in English until 1792. William Collins, James Thomson, Thomas Gray, and James Macpherson in his *Ossian*—the Romantic writers in the Age of Reason—were the contemporary poets she found most congenial, and Salvator Rosa and Claude Lorrain were clearly her favorite painters. Evidence from her work indicates that she was familiar with the popular moral philosophies of her day, as well as with the esthetic pronouncements of Samuel Johnson and Edmund Burke. While here and there she evidences liberal tendencies in both religion and politics, the tenor of her thought in all things was essentially conservative.

In 1787, she married William Radcliffe, a Londoner, an Oxonian, and a law student until he took up parliamentary reporting and journalism and still later became the proprietor of the *English Chronicle*. Their married life was ostensibly a happy one. Since Talfourd received his information about this happiness from William Radcliffe, gleanings from other sources need not be construed as scandal-mongering if they qualify Talfourd by suggesting that, at least during the 1790's, this childless marriage had its requisite ups and downs. Mrs. Radcliffe's mother had little confidence in her son-in-law's ability to handle money. When she died, she emphasized in her will that he was not to receive the slightest portion of the money she bequeathed to her daughter. The absolute lack of any correspondence from so easily a prolific writer as Mrs. Radcliffe is itself a curious anomaly in a time when the one legitimate literary expression allowed young ladies was the familiar exchange of thoughts provided by letter writing.

Anecdotage with a strained or intimated relevance to Mrs. Radcliffe's work confirms both the contemporary lack of real knowledge about her life and the understandable tendency of folk biographers to supply details which fit their preconceptions when, at any rate, there are no facts to frustrate their fancies. There is a tale, left darkly ominous in its suggestiveness, that unspeakable atrocities had been committed in a house close to the Ward residence in Bath. A related tale tells of a local family, locked up in their country house, that vanished finally into thin air—much like Ludovico in *The Mysteries of Udolpho*. Montague Summers retails the semihumorous account according to which Mrs. Radcliffe ate underdone pork chops before going to bed at night—so that the consequent nightmares might serve as substance for her novels.

A contemporary fable with a wider appeal—it imposed on Sir

Walter Scott for several years—related that the authoress, deranged by the horrors conceived by her gothicizing imagination, had been committed to a madhouse. Mrs. Radcliffe, though aware of some of these tales, found it equally offensive to her sense of propriety to deny publicly that she was mad or to affirm, in spite of published reports to the contrary, that she was still living, if not writing. Talfourd expends much space attempting to disprove an account of her actual death in 1823 which maintained that she had at last succumbed to brain fever, a consequence of a mind forever afflicting itself with horrible imaginings.

The relevance to her work and reputation of such apocrypha is that they were felt likely and significant enough to be perpetrated as natural *"expliqués"* of the mystery in which she chose to obscure her life from the public eye. Even the substantiated detail of her life stems largely from anecdotes carefully selected to explain her seclusion and to excuse her from the rather dubious distinction of being a novelist. From her semigenteel background, Talfourd says, she inherited an aversion to authorship and the kind of notoriety it brought with it. She wrote to amuse herself—an acceptable motive for whiling away one's lonely hours behind the pen—when her husband stayed late at the office. When he came home, she presented him with her evening's work, which "he could not read alone without shuddering." She laughed at his reaction and to depreciate her busy-work. Neither the vanity of authorship nor the meretriciousness of mere moneymaking took precedence over the decorously lighthearted spirit in which, so Talfourd implies, she wrote her novels.

The excessive sensibility she shared with her heroines is abundantly illustrated in her reactions to personal slights which offended "the delicacy of her mind," though unmotivated by any malice or spite in the persons responsible for them. A largely jocular comment by Scott concerning her Gothic machinery hurt her enough for Talfourd to wish that he had omitted the barb embedded in the jest. Mrs. Radcliffe was likewise offended at an editorial note in the published letters of Elizabeth Carter, poet, translator, and bluestocking, which, though far from saying it, intimated to Mrs. Radcliffe that Mrs. Carter had avoided her acquaintance. When advised after her death that Mrs. Radcliffe had so interpreted the note, the editor evidenced the delicate sense of propriety still extant in 1824 by apologizing for the intimation he had not implied.

The "singular apprehensiveness of her moral sense" was evoked when Mrs. Radcliffe discovered that Joanna Baillie's *Plays on the Passions* had been ascribed to her in Anna Seward's correspondence. She made every effort to discredit the rumor because she could not bear the thought of seeming to take credit for works not her own. Given the reason for the false ascription, we might suppose that she was at least as much offended by the rather telling criticism of her structural ineptitudes, dramatic improprieties, and descriptive excesses:

Before their author was known, I observed so much of the power and defects of Mrs. Radcliffe's compositions in these dramas as to believe them hers, and I hear she owns them. Mrs. Radcliffe, in whatever she writes, attentive solely to the end is not sufficiently attentive to observe probability in the means she uses to attain it. She bends her plan —or, if it will not bend, she breaks it—to her catastrophe by making it grow out of the preceding events. Still she always takes hold of the reader's feelings and effects her purpose boldly, if not regularly. Her descriptive talent, used to satiety in her novels, is here employed with more temperance and, consequently, to better purpose.[3]

Mrs. Seward's letter is dated May 21, 1799, or before Joanna Baillie had written those plays on the passions which would have best corresponded with the predominant Radcliffean passion—terror. In 1812 she published three plays delineating various occasions of and reactions to "Fear," with superstitious fears appropriately embodied in the reaction of a Radcliffean-type heroine.

Like the *expliqués* which pluck out the heart of the mysterious phenomena in her fictional second life, there seems to be a rational—and even prosaic—explanation for the obscurity in which she enveloped her private life by separating it from her public role as the leading novelist of the day. There was, first of all, the eighteenth-century view of the novel as, at best, a waste of time— if not, in fact, an invitation to immorality. The most significant female novelist before Ann Radcliffe and her contemporaries was the notorious Aphra Behn, whose writings were geared to the freewheeling and frank-speaking Restoration culture she represented. While the circulating libraries were instrumental in Mrs. Radcliffe's huge popular success, the customary provender with which they fed their ever-growing audience was nothing if not distasteful to the moralists of the day. Jane Austen's annoyed defense of the novel (in *Northanger Abbey*) against even the novel writer himself suggests by its tone and content the abject willingness with which the novelist generally expiated his practice by condemning it.

The most compelling reason for Mrs. Radcliffe's decision to stop writing at the height of her public and critical esteem was probably the kind of emulation this esteem prompted. A prim moralist, she could not tolerate the public image she was forced to share with her imitators who unconscionably added sex to her lily-white sensationalism and thereby eliminated the Radcliffean delicacy of sentiment which consistently saved her heroine from a fate worse than death. The audience of post-Radcliffean horror epics was titillated by ocular evidence of the heroine's deflowering. When Mrs. Radcliffe discovered the sensual subject matter in Matthew Lewis's *The Monk*—written in professed emulation of her *Udolpho* —she undertook to rub it out by (in effect) bowdlerizing the work in her next book, *The Italian*. While Talfourd assures us her mental stability held up under the onslaughts of her own gothicizing, a speculative reader may wonder how she would have reacted to the ultimate degradation of the Gothic sentimental heroine that the Marquis de Sade cynically delineated in his *Justine*. And de Sade was an admirer of Mrs. Radcliffe's work.

From the appearance of *The Romance of the Forest* (1791) through the critical appraisal of *The Italian* (1797), Mrs. Radcliffe experienced a popularity which no novelist before her—not Henry Fielding, not Samuel Richardson, not Tobias Smollett, nor Laurence Sterne—had come close to achieving. The £500 she received for *Udolpho* and the £800 she received for *The Italian* attest to one kind of popularity; the fact that the reviewers, whose praise was not always judicious or consistently principled, were seconded both by the bluestocking remnant and by men of sophisticated and serious interests like Charles Fox, Richard Sheridan, and Joseph Warton attest to another. But, when her fame threatened to degenerate into notoriety, she asserted her sense of values by retiring from public notice; and, so the story goes, she lived happily ever after. Other than this implicit moral indictment of her followers, the remaining relevant accounts of her life that aid in an understanding of her work appear in the descriptive passages of her *Journey through Holland, &c. Made in the Summer of 1794* and of the posthumously published excerpts from the diary notes jotted down during the many excursions she and her husband took around and after the turn of the century.[4]

II *Sentimental Journey*

The most significant event recorded in the Continental portion of the 1794 *Journey* concerns the Radcliffes' failure to cross into Switzerland because of the spiteful officiousness of a border guard. Mrs. Radcliffe was thereby denied her only chance of actually setting foot among scenic sublimities akin to those she had imaginatively passed through in her recently written *The Mysteries of Udolpho*. More relevant than what she missed seeing was what she could not resist describing when faced with a type of arbitrary authority whose effect on her capacity for terror was much like Montoni's on Emily's kindred sensibility: "He left us with a notice that we could not quit the town without receiving the Commandant's permission by his means; and it was with some terror that we perceived ourselves to be so much in his power, in a place where . . . the least expression of just indignation seemed to provoke a disposition for further injustice" (276).

Rather than parley with the guard, whom tactful perseverance would seemingly have mollified, she relied on the forebodings of her imagination, which "suggested . . . all the horror of oppression." With less courage than some of her heroines, she and her husband retraced their way to England. These imaginative terrors perhaps received expression a few years later in *The Italian*, as did the two German Capuchins, "gloomily sublime," whom she saw walking (like Schedoni) along the seashore at Boppart "wrapt in the long black drapery of their order, their heads shrouded in cowls that half concealed their faces" (310).

The gloomy sublimity of the Capuchins and the "horror of oppression" which Mrs. Radcliffe felt evidence her knowledge of the prevailing esthetic terminology of the day embodied in Edmund Burke's *Enquiry into the Origin of our Ideas of the Sublime and Beautiful*. Sublime feelings and the terror which often produced them were the high points of her Gothic art and were the chief emotional attributes of her Gothic heroine. The following distinction between horror and terror, in a dialogue originally intended for *Gaston de Blondeville*, indicates how closely Mrs.

Radcliffe knew her Burke and how aware she was of the precise gradations of fearful response she elicited from her heroine and, by extension, from her reader: "Terror and horror are so far opposite, that the first expands the soul and awakens the faculties to a high degree of life; the other contracts, freezes, and nearly annihilates them. I apprehend neither Shakespeare nor Milton by their fictions, nor Mr. Burke by his reasoning, anywhere looked to positive horror as a source of the sublime, though they all agree that terror is a very high one. . . ." [5]

The relevant portion of the *Journey*, like the diary excerpts in Talfourd's "Memoir," are concerned with Ann Radcliffe's reaction to the sublime, the beautiful, and the Gothic in the landscape and architecture which she saw in England. Like many contemporary travellers before and after her, she observed the landscape with an eye taught to discriminate among the natural features she passed through according to the rules of the picturesque. "English landscape," she says, "may be compared to cabinet pictures delicately beautiful and highly finished" (370).

She had read Burke and the landscape critics and compositors who warned against mixing the sublime and the beautiful indiscriminately. Nature's Landscape Artist is criticized, as a result, for mismatching scenic features at Derwentwater in the Lake District: "The water is too small for its accompaniments; and its form being round and seen entirely at once, leaves nothing for expectation to pursue beyond the stretching promontory, or fancy to transform within the gloom and obscurity of the receding fell; and thus it loses an ample source of the sublime. . . . The beauty of its banks, also, contending with the wildness of its rocks gives opposite impressions to the mind, and the force of each is perhaps destroyed by the admission of the other" (451). She continues to echo Burke —sublimity is rendered insignificant in the presence of too much beauty, since simplicity (or unity of effect) is one of its chief attributes. Like Burke, she emphasizes the psychological effect of the sublime which produces "a high tone of mind" and, when simply adorned, does not "jar upon the feelings."

Visiting Rydal Hall, Mrs. Radcliffe has a chance to pronounce on the work of the landscape planners who, in her view (likewise set forth in *The Mysteries of Udolpho*), should imbue their art with "graceful plainness and meek subjection to nature." She continues: "The taste by which a cascade in the pleasure-grounds, pouring under the arch of a rude bridge, amidst the green tint of woods, is shown through a darkened garden house, and therefore with all the effect which opposition of light and shade can give, is not too artificial; so admirably is the intent accomplished of making all the light that is admitted fall upon objects which are chiefly meant to be observed" (471).

Contrast and a decorous chiaroscuro highlight what an indiscriminate juxtaposition in art and an unfortunate mixture in nature either obscure or contradict. Mrs. Radcliffe so describes a pastoral scene in nature which could have come from a painting or from one of her novels: "Here, on the right, at the feet of awful rocks, was spread a gay autumnal scene, in which the peasants were singing merrily as they gathered the oats into sheafs; woods, turfy hillocks, and above all, tremendous crags, abruptly closing round the yellow harvest. The figures together with the whole landscape assembled one of those beautifully fantastic scenes which fable calls up before the wand of the magician" (416).

Years later, Thomas Love Peacock found grounds for some satire and caustic comment in the picturesque seekers' proclivity for seeing laborers as "figures" in a landscape rather than as people who were likely to be suffering from social and economic inequalities. For Mrs. Radcliffe, they are only functional insofar as they enhance the imaginative appeal of the landscape by animating it with the kind of human interest her esthetic sense requires. As her *Journey* indicates, she was by no means unsympathetic to the plight of the poor; she had a contemporary facility for seeing the beauty as well as the poverty of their lot.

A pertinent appeal to her reader's imagination is couched in an interpolated admission of the inadequacy of words to distinguish the varying scenery she is passing through: "A repetition of the same images of rock, wood, and water, and the same epithets of grand, vast, and sublime, which necessarily occur, must appear tautologous on paper, though their archetypes in nature, ever varying in outline or arrangement, exhibit new visions to the eye and produce new shades of effect on the mind" (419). The apology could stand as an implicit footnote to the redundant nature descriptions of *The Romance of the Forest* and *The Mysteries of Udolpho*. But the fact that innumerable such journals devoted to little else but natural description received extensive coverage and discriminating praise from the reviewers indicates that the imaginations of her contemporaries were primed to fill in the individualized detail she could not write into her descriptions.

Ullswater, which she rates the most sublime and therefore esthetically the most affecting among the major lakes, conveys the impression of "vast power and astonishing majesty." Power, merging with suggestive obscurity and a sense of the artificial infinite, produces an effect on her which Wordsworth will soon corroborate in *The Prelude*'s account of his childhood experiences in the same locale; for Mrs. Radcliffe wrote: "The effect of Ullswater is that, awful as its scenery appears, it awakens the mind to expectation still more awful, and touching all the powers of imagination inspires that 'fine phrensy' descriptive of the poet's eye, which not only bodies forth unreal forms, but imparts to substantial objects a character higher than their own" (477).

The particular kind of "expectation still more awful" aroused in her heroines in kindred settings may lead to thoughts of God, or to the "solemn and delightful emotion" which the "sentimental beauty" of Furness Abbey and its ancient trees inspires in her, or to Gothic visions of "witches . . . at their incantations, calling spirits from the clouds and spectres from the earth"—a Shakespearean fancy which Mrs. Radcliffe indulged near Keswick. The "almost supernatural . . . gloom and sublimity" of Ullswater is set off against the "fantastic wildness and romantic beauty" of Derwentwater and the mere "prettinesses" which describe the islands breaking up the sublime effect which vast expanses of water achieve in their bare simplicity or when inlaid, as Windermere is, with only a single large island.

The Burkean suggestiveness implicit in her clichéd vocabulary of the picturesque was calculated to evoke in her reader expansive associations such as she imported into an 1805 visit to Belvedere House:

In a shaded corner, near the chimney, a most exquisite Claude, an evening view, perhaps over the Campagna of Rome. The sight of this picture imparted much of the luxurious repose and satisfaction which we derive from contemplating the finest scenes of nature. Here was the poet, as well as the painter, touching the imagination and making you see more than the picture contained. You saw the real light of the sun, you breathed the air of the country, you felt all the circumstances of a luxurious climate on the most serene and beautiful landscape;

and, the mind being thus softened, you almost fancied you heard Italian music on the air—the music of Paisello; and such, doubtless, were the scenes that inspired him. ("Memoir," 65)

If her reader works as sympathetically with her as she does with Claude, similar verbal transcriptions in her novels likewise re-create the life of a landscape even to the music in the air, which floats into the appropriate scenic decor amidst a mind-softening silence.

Her associations go beyond Burkean suggestiveness, which is inextricably involved with some species of the terribly obscure, to Deistic invocations of nature's God much like those her female characters give vent to when oppressed by villains or simply impressed by the scenery. Like her Emily in *The Mysteries of Udolpho* she recalls her dead parents in the midst of a sublime landscape whose "melancholy greatness" assured her both of her mortal fate and her consequent resurrection: "Oh GOD! thy great laws will one day be more fully known by thy creatures . . . ," and so on. Such prayers were doubtless conventional indulgences, but they were *felt* conventions, much as the occasions for sentimental effusions in the sensibility novels and dramas were felt to the point of tears by audiences conditioned to respond to them. When on another occasion a grand display of the elements frightens her, she again lives out her role as a Radcliffean heroine by disinterestedly subliming away her personal fears to envision it all as a dramatic "token of God directing his world" (53).

A more ambivalent view of the religious sublime appears in her *Journey* treatment of nuns and monks, convents and monasteries. When visiting a nunnery whose inmates had taken the vow of silence, the very thought of the sublimely macabre austerity of their lives made "her blood thrill and teeth chatter." Her heroines are similarly afflicted, though Mrs. Radcliffe is more baroque and less naïve in imagining their reactions than she is in recording her own. Not long after this appropriately esthetic shudder at the expense of the silent nuns, she illustrates the impartiality of her reactions by praising a good monk she met at Bonn.

The general view of Catholicism in England during her time was imbued with stereotyped intolerance similar to that which characterized the Elizabethan attitude toward the Jew. Though conservative enough not to offend contemporary prejudices, Mrs.

Radcliffe could not resist the esthetic and ethical impulse to qualify her harsher criticisms of "the thunders of the Vatican and all the terrors of the Inquisition" with a saving and spontaneous avowal of their occasional sublimity and of the rarer deviations into justice that their dispensations were sometimes redeemed by. As Gothic decor, monks and nuns were both esthetically exotic and ethically dangerous; for both were relics and living ghosts of the medieval era to which she traced their habits and their sentiments. In the *Journey*, she neatly sums up her ambivalence and its source when she comments on the ruined monasteries of the Lake District: "though reason rejoices that they no longer exist, the eye may be allowed to regret" (411).

The *Journey* description of Brougham Castle and the diary account of Kenilworth Castle are the major parallels, if not sources, in her travels for the inanimate proponent who provides the customary backdrop for her persecuted heroine's real and imaginary terrors—the castle itself: "Dungeons, secret passages and heavy iron rings remain to hint of unhappy wretches who were perhaps rescued only by death from these horrible engines of a tryrant's will. The bones probably of such victims are laid beneath the damp earth of these vaults" (427).

If such bones do not rest under Brougham Castle, they certainly have a place under Udolpho. "One almost saw the surly keeper descending through this door-case and heard him rattle the keys . . . , listening with indifference to the clank of chains and to the echo of that groan which seemed to rend the heart it burst from." Vivaldi is soon to hear that very groan in the chambers of the Inquisition—and neither he nor his readers will be less apt at sympathizing with its implications than Ann Radcliffe is here. When she later "mounted a perilous stair-case, of which many steps were gone, and others trembled to the pressure," she must have recalled passing that way before—with Ferdinand in *The Sicilian Romance*.

Verbal parallels and ghostly allusions indicate that Mrs. Radcliffe's visit to Kenilworth Castle inspired her posthumously published historical romance *Gaston de Blondeville*. *Ubi sunt* reflections elicited by a ruined banquet hall entwined with dead ivy stalks (which "seemed to crawl about the ruin in sympathy") recall *The Romance of the Forest* and work their way into *Gaston*: "generations have beheld us and passed away, as you now behold us and shall pass away . . . yet we remain . . . " ("Memoir," 58).

Moving through the Gothic chapel of the castle to its Gothic armory, she is well primed for the object she sees and the associations she makes: "A large figure in complete armour, the beaver down, and a sword in its hand! The general twilight, with the last western gleam touching the bronze, gave full effect to this scene, and heightened the obscurity of the stairs, in perspective. This armour came from Germany; our conductor knew no more" (Memoir," 59).

The perspective is not only at Kenilworth but in memory and imagination. It is her favorite time for contrasted scenic decor—the twilight just fading in the West and the sun's rays striking some barren crag or dark tower in one last eerie chiaroscuro. The play for rhetorical effect at the end of the passage echoes similar laconic sentences in her novels whose real purpose is not to satisfy curiosity but to tempt it toward ominous imaginative inference. Possibly the knight was put into motion, black with his beaver down, when, predictably, Mrs. Radcliffe was reminded of her favorite scene from *Hamlet*: "Before these great gates and underneath these towers, Shakespeare's ghost might have stalked . . ." ("Memoir," 60). *Gaston de Blondeville* is the only novel in which Mrs. Radcliffe does not explain her ghost away.

Exact verbal parallels confirm the influence of the Kenilworth visit on *Gaston*. However, in almost all other instances, parallels between descriptions in the *Journey* or "Memoir" and in the novels are worth noting but not pressing. The value of such source hunting is seriously diminished by the provable irrelevance of an ideally congruent description. Mrs. Seward notes in a 1796 letter that a *Journey* description of Mary Stuart's room at Hardwicke might have suggested a parallel description in *Udolpho*, but the visit came after the novel. Scott likewise assumed that Udolpho's scenic decor stemmed from the *Journey* Rhine trip because of parallel terminology.

An alternative assumption, given such balked sources, is that Mrs. Radcliffe tended to see real castles and scenery with the same imaginative eye that envisioned their counterparts in the novels. The descriptive rhetoric of the picturesque was then drawn on to supplement and re-create not only what the writer imagined in art but also what she saw in nature. By her own admission Mrs. Radcliffe fashioned her *Journey* and diary landscapes into generalized verbal patterns which blended subtly discriminated scenes in nature into vaguely redundant contrasts of the sublime and beautiful in words. Only when describing minute objects in nature—tufts of flowers—does she bother specifying their distinctive streaks and contours.

A semi-Gothic reflection at the Sydney residence in Penshurst rises to a visionary mood like Wordsworth's on Sarum Plain before it dwindles into the picturesque:

The rafters have been blackened by the fires of two centuries, lighted on the centre of the pavement, where the bricks, raised half a foot, form a small octagon on which, perhaps, Sir Philip Sydney and the knights his companions have often stood round the blazing faggots. . . . I think I see, in glimpses, the strong blaze of the wood flashing on their visages. The armour of Sir Philip himself . . . stands at the back of an obscure gallery and close beneath a high window, whose small frames admit a blunted, melancholy light. It stands like a spectre in arms, watching over the scene it once inhabited; and is admirably placed to touch the imagination, but not to gratify curiosity, its distance being considerable. A partial light, thrown more strongly on the head, would give a very fine effect. ("Memoir," 83)

The descripition is much more vivid and detailed than comparable scenes in her novels. But the critical conclusion illustrates both her dramatic sense of the sublime and her verbal-pictorial methods of achieving it. Key descriptions and incidents in her novels first "touch" on the imagination, but they are sufficiently distanced by vagueness or the lack of empirical detail to keep curiosity unsatisfied. The reader's imagination is incited to probe but never to dissolve the darkness or to diminish the distance until the author gives him a little light or lets him come a little closer.

While on rare occasions the travel journals present an Ann Radcliffe refreshingly open to humor and interested in the commonplace, her projected image generally reflects the personae of her novels. Her esthetic reactions confirm the moral implications of the parabolic anecdotes her husband put at Talfourd's disposal. She was as exquisitely sensitive to the sublime in nature and in Gothic edifices as she was to the proprieties of social life and to the possible impropriety of novel writing. When she did "publish herself" (in Talfourd's phrase), she did it warily and with an eye to the ideal. Her audience expected no less from her. When her readers exchanged their fictional heroine for a feminine lead in a real-life situation, they expected the living lady to portray the virtues of the heroine. Knowing something of Mrs. Radcliffe's moral and esthetic sensibility, the modern reader knows what to expect in the works of a novelist who lived up to what she wrote about.

Time Magazine April 22, 1966
Bettman Archives

ANN RADCLIFFE

CHAPTER 2

The Gothic Background

I The Supernatural

THE instinctive fear of the supernatural which is tacitly assumed by the Gothic novelist as part of his reader's psychological makeup was appealed to by Homer when he recounted Odysseus's visit to the Underworld. A few centuries later, the unknown author of the Book of Job provided his hero with precisely the kind of reaction an engaged Gothic reader (like Henry Tilney) indulged when he read of supernatural phenomena like those experienced by Job: "In thoughts from the visions of the night, when deep sleep falleth upon men, fear came upon me and trembling, which made all my bones to shake. Then a spirit passed before my face. The hair on my flesh stood up. It stood still, but I could not discern the form thereof; an image was before mine eyes; there was silence; and I heard a voice . . ." (iv, 13–17). The gloomy shades and dismal visitants Odysseus encounters and the palpable terror which afflicts Job are familiar anticipations of the more direct literary sources of English Gothicism in Elizabethan and Jacobean drama. Less known but comparable anticipations appear in writers as important, various, and "classical" as Herodotus, Sophocles, Dante, and even Chaucer. Shakespeare, Cyril Tourneur, John Webster, and their contemporaries evoked the terror Aristotle had prescribed as basic to the tragic catharsis by conjuring up not only ghosts of the ostensibly departed dead but also bloody-minded and -handed villains whose actions supplemented supernatural horrors with human atrocities.

Walpole's Otranto was antedated in English fiction by a few sporadic forays into Gothic territory, but such efforts were invariably subordinate to the main thrust of the novels in which they appeared. Smollett's picaresque *Ferdinand Count Fathom* (1753) is the sole distinctive precursor of Walpole's work. Probably because Smollett's concern with the psychology of fear was more subtle than Walpole's, his Gothic interpolations—banditti, intrusive corpses, graveyards at midnight, ghostly apparitions, and even the consequent *expliqué*—anticipate in their hair-raising effects the detailed Radcliffean accounts of an acutely sensitized subject immersed in an atmosphere of dark foreboding and blood-congealing innuendo. But Smollett's lurid sidelights on the supernatural, though significantly marked by his genius, are incidental when they occur; for they are detached features of his novel rather than organic to the picaresque motive which inspired it.

"The Graveyard School" of English poetry did more than Smollett to keep alive for mid-eighteenth-century English sensibilities the features of the horrific sublime which had been much curtailed by the advent of Reason and its gospel of common sense. With a distinguished precedent in John Milton's *Il Penseroso,* writers like Thomas Parnell ("Night Piece on Death," 1722), David Mallet ("Excursion," 1728), Edward Young ("Night Thoughts on Life, Death and Immortality," 1742), and Robert Blair ("The Grave," 1743) interweave their didactic themes with an appropriately somber pattern full of hooting owls, flitting bats, twilight-to-midnight settings, the requisite graveyard, and, everywhere, melancholy emblems of death that emphasize the transience and vanity of life. This psychomasochistic reveling in gloomy contemplation of *memento mori* is an emphatic precursor of the "not unpleasing melancholy" without which no Gothic heroine was temperamentally suited to her role. The sublime, the sentimental, the macabre, and the gloomy context in nature, which become the stock features of the Gothic romance, contribute to the recurrent accoutrements of these poems in a synthesis close enough to suggest a direct descent from the poetry to the novel.

Translations of the *Arabian Nights* tales in the early part of the eighteenth century at first inspired writers—like Joseph Addison (in *The Spectator* and *The Guardian*) and, later, like Samuel Johnson (*Rasselas,* 1759) and Oliver Goldsmith (*The Citizen of the World,* 1762)—to use Oriental fantasy as a framework for moral, philosophical, and political satire with something of the distancing perspective provided in *Gulliver's Travels.* Such works helped condition the reading public for the extravagances of later pseudo-Oriental narratives full of genii, magicians, and bands of fairy folk in whose company a mere human being dwindled into nonentity.

William Beckford's *Vathek* is the crowning glory of the Oriental tale, though its publication in 1786 also served to indicate that the human sentiments necessary to sustain reader interest could not be built into a novel whose primary base was in an unreal world where motivation was largely a matter of whimsy. In spite of a magnificently somber Gothic conclusion, the tone set in *Vathek* when the villain rolls into a ball to be kicked from Vathek's palace generally keeps the reader aware that an occasional ascent into the sublime is only an accidental deviation from the ridiculous inconsequence that patterns the novel as a whole. The fact that *Vathek* did not initiate any serious competition to the Gothic novel during the 1790's indicates that not only the discriminating reading public, as represented by the reviewers, but even and eventually the lower ranks of the common reader came to demand more relevant human identification in their reading fare than they found in the thin and insubstantial fabric of Oriental fantasy. They wanted a supernatural somehow humanized by credible emotional involvements in situations where moral decisions were feasible.

They found this combination in the Gothic novel, though the first and, for some, the greatest of these was not much less imbued with fantasy—or much more with human interest—than *Vathek*. *The Castle of Otranto* symbolizes a century's need for a species of emotional expression which was denied only at the risk of incurring the malaise which the novel itself symptomizes. Common sense, which mediated between reason and empiricism in artistic circles, had fairly well nullified the esthetic effect of a Shakespearean ghost by equating it with barbarism, enthusiasm, superstition, and irreligion. While the dread of the supernatural was thereby rationalized from contemporary art, it was by no means rationalized out of mind—nor, in the fugitive underchurnings of "graveyard poetry," did it ever lack an outlet even in art for a displaced and sublimated expression. But in such poems the moral and religious didacticism was meant to overlay and justify the supernatural machinery and its Gothic suggestion. As a significant public figure in a hyperrational society, Walpole was ideally situated to illustrate its emotionally repressive sanctions by discarding them when he left Parliament for his Gothic castle at Strawberry Hill. And not only did he refuse to apologize for the exuberant irrationality of his supernatural effects, but years later, when Clara Reeve rationalized them away in *The Old English Baron,* he was vociferously outraged at what he conceived to be her perversion of his art.

The famous description of the dream in which *Otranto* had its origin is surrealistic in form; but, as Walpole notes, in content it is a completely natural product of a subconscious mind drawing on daydreams and denying an unsympathetic reality:

I waked one morning in the beginning of last June from a dream, of which all I could recover was that I had thought myself in an ancient castle (a very natural dream for a head filled, like mine, with Gothic story) and that, on the uppermost bannister of a great staircase, I saw a gigantic hand in armour. In the evening I sat down and began to write, without knowing in the least what I intended to say or relate. The work grew in my hands, and I grew fond of it. Add that I was very glad to think of anything rather than politics. In short, I was so engrossed with my tale, which I completed in less than two months, that one evening I wrote from the time I had drank my tea, about six o'clock, till half an hour after one in the morning, when my hand and fingers were so weary that I could not hold the pen to finish the sentence, but left Matilda and Isabella talking in the middle of a paragraph.[1]

The extravagance of the tale itself also testifies to the strictness of the rational expectations, in art as in life, which Walpole completely disregarded when it occurred to him to relax them at all. The diabolical villain, the sentimental heroine, the peasant-prince—such stock features of the fairy tale and the sentimental romance barely bring to earth and humanize the huge helmet that crushes a prospective bridegroom, the gigantic hand itself, and the other portions and signs of a giant presence distributed here and there in castle and courtyard. While the story hardly matters, the typically Gothic features deserve notice because of their innumerable repetitions and variations in the novels of the 1790's. There is the bleeding statue, the ragged skeleton, the inevitable birth-mark proving significant kinship, the castle itself, its labyrinthine corridors made for a heroine's endless and terror-stricken flights, a cleric and his church—and everywhere darkness, gusty winds and flickering candles. Added to these is Walpole's occasional attempt at fulfilling his prefatory promise by uniting with the fairy tale and the chivalric romance the sentimental attitudes and pathos variously developed in the latter-day heroic romance and in the novel of sensibility.

Conceivably, Walpole might have expected his work to have had an effect on the critical sensibilities of his time that was as shattering as the giant helmet when it landed in the midst of Otranto's courtyard. "I have composed it," he wrote, "in defiance of rules, of critics, and of philosophers." [2] In fact, the reaction was mixed and qualified; for the critics were apparently puzzled and at times alienated by the extravagances perpetrated in the name of medieval romance. They were, however, mollified by the sentiments and by the moral tone of character and outcome which the contemporary novel had conditioned them to locate and praise even when these qualities were relatively negligible.

It was thirteen years before *Otranto* was recast and decorously emulated by Clara Reeve in *The Champion of Virtue* (1777), which better fulfilled its subtitle *A Gothic Story* when it was republished in 1778 as *The Old English Baron*. Mrs. Reeve explicitly stated that she intended to fulfill Walpole's poorly executed attempt at combining the medieval romance and the modern novel. She discovered the reason for Walpole's failure to produce an esthetically attractive combination of the old and the new in his misuse or overuse of "violent machinery," which "destroys the effect it is intended to produce." [3] The indicated antidote to the palling effect which *Otranto* had on the reader's mind was, she said, to reduce the sensational to a minimum and to restrict it within "the utmost verge of probability." Walpole's derision of her attempt to bowdlerize his work helped establish the opposed views of the Gothic novel which the critics and the writers themselves were to advocate and illustrate during the next fifty years. The question was simple, but it remained a moot one: should supernatural phenomena be explained away or should they be allowed to retain their supernatural status in the face of reason, empirical evidence, and (perhaps) morality and religion?

Mrs. Reeve's recipe for a palatable combination of the ancient romance and the modern novel contains the bare formula for Radcliffean Gothic, but it lacks the flavoring of the sublime and the suspenseful which Mrs. Radcliffe's more comprehensive synthesis included: "there is required a sufficient degree of the marvellous to excite the attention; enough of the manners of real life to give an air of probability to the work; and enough of the pathetic to engage the heart in its behalf." [4] Supernatural phenomena "reduced to reason and probability" might have betrayed Walpole's cathartic purpose. They were, however, precisely what the public wanted—in just the form they wanted it. There were thirteen editions of Mrs. Reeve's novel in the nine years after its initial publication as *The Champion of Virtue.* The Gothic title likely sold more copies than the austerely moral original would have done, but the implications of the earlier title are both borne out in the work and were apparently gratifying—or perhaps solacing—to readers who might have felt uncomfortable with the thought that their reading time was spent more for pleasure than for profit.

Of the remaining domestic anticipations of the Gothic inundation during the 1790's, only Sophia Lee's *The Recess* (1785) contained the pleasing combination of supernatural suggestions and a sentimental heroine or two to suffer their emotional consequences. The "recess" is a well-accommodated demi-cave in which two supposititious daughters of Mary, Queen of Scots, are reared in secret until the time comes—as it does to all sentimental heroines during their late teens—to meet a set of lovers with whom they exchange vows, tears, and tragedy.

Mrs. Radcliffe was most likely familiar with Miss Lee's book, as she was with the much more prolific output of another contemporary, Mrs. Charlotte Smith, whose productive years fairly well coincide with those of Mrs. Radcliffe. Mrs. Smith's best book, *The Old Manor House* (1793), is not only full of sentiment and ably conceived Gothic situations but also contains distinctive scenic decor reminiscent of Mrs. Radcliffe's then recently published *Romance of the Forest* and prophetic of *The Mysteries of Udolpho.* While Mrs. Smith slightly anticipated Mrs. Radcliffe in the descriptive and Gothic techniques they shared, the likelihood is that the success of each during the 1790's made the influence reciprocal. However, Mrs. Radcliffe never acquired Mrs. Smith's talent for characterization and comic interlude, nor did Mrs. Smith typically emulate for its own sake the meticulous development of suspenseful and terrific occasions that became synonymous with Radcliffean Gothic.

Because of various cognate sources—in Elizabethan drama, "graveyard poetry," and the early sentimental novel in England—it is difficult to assess in a brief space the precise influence that relevant eighteenth-century German and French writings had on the developing strain of English Gothic. Perhaps the safest generalization about possible influences back and forth across the Channel is that none of the literatures involved required any of the others as a source for the major elements they possessed in common. England, at any rate, did not require the aid it nonetheless received.

While the German chivalric, "robber," and horror romances contained the requisite features of a medieval setting, daring and dangerous banditti, plus ghosts, monks, dungeons, and crumbling towers, their earliest author, Schiller, was predated by *Otranto*. It was not until 1781 that his play *Die Räuber* was published. Though its influence when translated during the 1790's was great —the major English Romantic poets were particularly impressed by it—its inspiration, according to Samuel Taylor Coleridge, came from Richardson's *Clarissa* and from Young's *Night Thoughts*. The influx of the various breeds of German Gothic was in fact contemporaneous with the mainstream of the Gothic tendency that welled from a virtually unadulterated domestic source. The single most apparent acknowledgment of German prestige among the English novel-reading public was the countless "tales from the German" emanating from the Minerva Press, whose editors did not balk at ascribing a German source to a domestic product.

As for the French, both Antoine (Abbé) Prévost and Jean Jacques Rousseau undoubtedly added greatly to the flow of tears running freely through the more psychologically complex of the Gothic novels. But exaggerated sensibility was likewise English in origin, for Richardson was the prime mover behind the easily motivated sentiments of the Gothic heroine. Nonetheless, the contributing influence of the French was stronger than that of the Germans. The French heroic romance of the late seventeenth century—full of chivalry and stilted emotions—anticipated both the medieval revival and the sentimental interests of the modern novel. Prévost and, more impressively, his successor Baculard d'Arnaud not only abetted sentimental tendencies but clearly anticipated Gothic glooms and terrors. Writing about the time of *Otranto*, d'Arnaud offers a sophisticated rationale for Gothic terror by arguing that the writer-magician is inspired to create an illusion which expands the readers' imaginations beyond the bounds of mere humanity and its routine concerns. His relevant works are well-forested, castled, dungeoned, "corpsed," "graveyarded," dark, and blood-curdling. Yet, as he admits, Milton and Young were among his sources for the terrific sublime. In sum, English Gothicism in the 1790's drew its vigor and substance from native literary antecedents that at times took the indirect route of Continental emulation before making their way back home again.

By the last half of the eighteenth-century all that was lacking for a full-fledged avowal of a "Gothic sensibility" was a name, a rationale, and, if possible, a sense of tradition to establish its legitimacy. The critical appraisal of the word which was to name the sensibility varied from its mid-eighteenth-century definition as "a term of reproach, synonymous with barbarous, lawless, and tawdry," to its gradual reclassification—along with "enthusiasm" and "romantic"—among those words which connoted esthetic and imaginative merit. Clara Reeve called her *English Baron* a "Gothic" story because it "was a picture of Gothic times and manners." The medieval setting customarily incorporated the sentimental attributes which Mrs. Reeve assigned to it, though the burgeoning appeal of sheer sensationalism ultimately required commentators to specify precisely what kind of "Gothic novel" they were talking about.

An explicit rationale and genealogy of the "Gothic" in literature was written by Bishop Hurd and published in 1762 as *Letters on Chivalry and Romance*. His title implies both his subject matter and the source of his defense. He finds warrant for Gothic writing in Shakespeare, Edmund Spenser, and Milton; and he decided that adverse critics of Gothic and Romantic art set up standards that do not apply to the sublimity and magic which the greatest poets have incorporated into their works. Neoclassical standards of artistic perfection are by definition incompetent to decide the merits of an art whose end is to transcend any kind of limitation, including perfection.

Along with Joseph and Thomas Warton, Bishop Hurd helped provide a sympathetic critical environment for the medieval revival which was signalized by the publication of Thomas Percy's *Reliques of Ancient English Poetry* in 1765, a year after the appearance of *Otranto*. The antiquarian research evidenced by Bishop Percy's compendium of English and Scottish ballads did not extend to scrupulous scholarship, as the general acceptance of James Macpherson's and Thomas Chatterton's forgeries proved.

The Gothic Background

But Macpherson's *Ossian* and Chatterton's Thomas Rowley poems elicited something more than scholarship: they elicited enthusiasm in their readers and, conceivably, in the fair share of the literate world willing to argue their authenticity exclusive of proof. Empirical evidence and rational inference were becoming suspect in the regions of art, where sublimity and feeling were the criteria for esthetic truth. Johnson put down the defender of Ossian's authenticity who asked whether any man living in the mid-eighteenth century could have composed such a work. Yes, Sir, said Johnson, any man, woman, or child. Johnson's questioner failed to sense the incipient spirit of the age, and Johnson himself failed to recognize its merit and significance.

For the common reader during the 1790's, "Gothic" was synonymous with terror, either actual or potential, both in what they read and what they felt. The synonym has stuck, though it is hardly a fair index to the many elements that went into the composition of Radcliffean Gothic. In order to appreciate Mrs. Radcliffe's novels and their comprehensive contemporary appeal it is necessary to have more than a glancing acquaintance with the ingredients of the sensibility novel, the esthetic of the sublime, and the cult of the picturesque in painting, in landscaping, and, most of all, in Nature.

II *Sentiment and Sensibility*

Eighteenth-century English philosophers as diverse in their premises as the third earl of Shaftesbury (Anthony Ashley Cooper) and David Hume or Francis Hutcheson and David Hartley generalized a relationship between the sense of beauty and the moral sensibility which English writers had been tacitly assuming since Shakespeare. The ethical optimism of Shaftesbury, which posited an essentially disinterested instinct in man that led him to harmonize his own interests with society's, was the moral equivalent of his esthetic assurance that beauty and truth were one. The emotional fervor of his prose style was the outward sign of his inner assurance. Ideally, moral beauty and esthetic beauty were inseparable predicates of each other. Feeling was regarded as a means of insight; intense feeling was indeed a criterion of belief and, hopefully, also of truth. Altruistic feeling, or sympathy, was the primal integrating emotion which linked together moral and esthetic sensibility.[5]

Adam Smith in his *Treatise on Moral Sentiments* locates sympathy in the imagination. In an example particularly appropriate to readers bent on weeping with their favorite sentimental heroines, Smith describes a hypothetical case of imaginative sympathy functioning disinterestedly and therefore morally: "By the imagination we place ourselves in his [a man on the rack's] situation, we conceive ourselves enduring all the same torments, we enter as it were into his body and become in some measure him, and thence form some ideas of his sensations, and even feel something which, though weaker in degree, is not altogether unlike them." [6]

The precise extent to which sympathy may become identity through the mediumship of "ideas" is indicated by the empirical reduction of personality to nothing more than a bundle of sensations variously reflected on by different individuals. Through a sympathetic attunement with the man on the rack—or the heroine in flight—we become that individual as we suffer through his sensations. The degree to which we can lose our objective identity in such a case (and insofar as we can be said to have one) is directly proportional to the capacity of our moral sensibility.

The job of the sentimental novelist, as d'Arnaud phrased it, was "to nourish and strengthen that sensibility which elevates man above the other creatures." Reason, he says, is not a sufficient distinction: "We must continually evidence that feeling, so precious and so affecting, by which we appropriate to ourselves the sufferings of our fellow-men." [7] And he justifies and praises the tears of sensibility that we shed for others, for they are the hallmark of our humanity and the warrant of our goodness.

Consequently, the moral capacity of a novel heroine is indexed by the quantity of her tears and the character of the occasions which elicit them. The reader profits in kind, accordingly as he identifies with her passion. Since there is no particular merit in identifying with pleasurable feelings, as usually defined, the moral end of a sentimental novel could only be served if its esthetic means were largely a matter of painful emotional extremities undergone, most appropriately, by the heroine. Aristotle's cathartic esthetic was revamped in philosophical essays and in chapters entitled "Agreeable feelings derived from painful incidents"—or words to like effect. The Burkean sublime, rooted in self-preservation, was characterized by terror—a "delightful" terror which was often induced by a sympathetic participation in the trials of others.

This esthetic of pain, vicariously endured, nourished the growth of a sentimental hypocrisy among readers who responded to the merest swoon of a heroine in order to prove to themselves and to others how much their sensibility was elevated above that of the other creatures. Such hypocrisy might have been morally detrimental if the readers had identified with what they read as profoundly as certain critics and satirists seemed to think they did. The real disservice was not to society's morals but to its literature. While writers were eventually shamed into discriminating gush from goodness, the equation between tears and virtue had become a critical formula which served as a golden rule for the great majority of novelists and reviewers until well into the 1790's.

Four years before Ann Radcliffe published her first novel, Clara Reeve, whose *Old English Baron* likely inspired Mrs. Radcliffe as much as it outraged Walpole, distinguished between "romance" and "novel" before getting to the real purpose of her *Progress of Romance*, which was to evaluate the esthetic merit of a book according to its ethical tone:

The Romance is an heroic fable, which treats of fabulous persons and things. The Novel is a picture of real life and manners, and of the times in which it is written. The Romance in lofty and elevated language describes what never happened nor is likely to happen.—The Novel gives a familiar relation of such things as pass every day before our eyes, such as may happen to a friend or to ourselves; and the perfection of it is to represent every scene in so easy and natural a manner, and to make them appear so probable, as to deceive us into a persuasion (at least while we are reading) that all is real, until we are afflicted by the joys or distresses of the person in the story as if they were our own.[8]

She not only suggests the combination of novel and romance which Walpole had attempted and she herself had illustrated, but intimates the more profound combination of natural passion and supernatural incident which Coleridge joined in "The Rime of the Ancient Mariner" and later justified in the *Biographia Literaria*.

But here Clara Reeve is only tangentially concerned with the innovative synthesis that she and Walpole instituted. After noting with approval the use of "Gothic imagery" in Spenser and Milton, she undertakes to discriminate among novels and romances according to their moral influence on the young who are the anticipated readers. *The Princess of Cleves*, a French heroic romance, is criticized by her because it encourages young minds "to plead errors of imagination for faults of the heart which, if indulged, will undermine both their virtue and their peace." Prévost's *Life of Cleveland* is considered to be "too much of the marvellous kind," but some scenes are "very pathetic . . . and above all other merit it has a moral tendency" (123).

After quoting a French eulogy on Richardson which calls him the most perfect interpreter and legislator of the human heart, Euphrasia, Mrs. Reeve's spokeswoman, says that she would want "no other criterion of a *good* or *bad* heart than the manner in which a young person was affected by reading *Pamela*" (135). When someone rather sensibly objects to Richardson's unsupportable prolixity and its esthetic effect on young girls who are thereby taught to "wiredraw" their language, Euphrasia disdainfully refers him to an "Epitome" of Richardson's novels, warning him, however, that "the pathetic addresses to the heart" have "evaporated" along with the tears that accompanied them.

The tedious procession of ideal heroes moving tepidly and facelessly through the representative sentimental novels is sanctioned in a Johnsonian reproof of Fielding for painting "human nature *as it is* rather than as *it ought to be*." Mixed characters in novels like Fielding's *Tom Jones* are bad because they seem to offer an escape for young readers who are not inclined to rigorously undeviating moral behavior. Wit, or imagination, is inevitably subordinated to morality by Mrs. Reeve, with a consequent leveling of purely esthetic values: "The dullest book that ever was written with a moral view is preferable to the most witty and elegant where these distinctions are overthrown" (II, 95). Circulating libraries, Rousseauistic morality, unorthodox religious views, and questioning of parental authority are all censured by like criteria. Significantly, Mrs. Reeve points out the misleading tendency of an overly sentimentalized heroine whose rather shoddy principles may be overlooked by that heroine's tears. Though Mrs. Reeve dismays the common reader when she praises *Otranto*, Thomas Leland's slightly Gothic *Longsword* (1762), and Smollett in general for their "moral tendency," she is being quite consistent with the ethical bias of her underlying esthetic principles. Perhaps to illustrate the relative mildness of her own censures, she concludes by quoting an anonymous but more violent defender of virtue as the prime esthetic, who would, he says, sooner hang an immoral writer than a thief. *The Progress of Romance* defines a specimen attitude toward pathos and morality that conditions and explains the practice which Mrs. Radcliffe conscientiously observed throughout her five Gothic novels.

Edith Birkhead, in her "Sentiment and Sensibility in the Eighteenth Century Novel" (1925), makes a convenient and useful distinction between the respective attitudes of Richardson and Sterne toward the sentimental novel which their names became synonymous with.[9] For Richardson, the novel was a semiallegorical vehicle of moral instruction. The tears and fears of the heroine (or hero) in a morally destructive environment were the outward signs of a perennial struggle which a middle-class young lady (the indicated audience) could identify with and learn from. Richardson admittedly idealized his heroines so that he could better display the moral attributes they possessed and the impossible resolution they maintained in the face of trial and temptation. Richardson's Clarissa is badgered on one hand by a family of arbitrary, narrow-principled self-seekers whose insensitivity appropriately conditions and sets off the extreme anguish they cause her. On the other hand, there is Lovelace, a lover whose passion exceeds his principles and finally rides roughshod over Clarissa's. Over a million words went into the telling of Clarissa's triumphant tragedy, relatively few of which were concerned with advancing a plot or adumbrating a tale. The changes rung on her moral sensibility make up the stuff and action of the fable.

Before Clara Reeve, Samuel Johnson made a trenchant distinction between story and sentiment in the novel which not only indexes Richardson's purpose but the kindred one of writers who paved the way for the sentimental emphasis of Radcliffean Gothic. Reading Richardson for the story, Johnson said, would so exhaust one's patience "that you would hang yourself . . . you must read him for the sentiment and consider the story as only giving occasion to the sentiment."[10] Melancholy rather than tragic pathos is generally the sentiment to which the story gives occasion. The "chère et delicieuse tristesse" which imbued Prévost's heroines with their poignancy and charm for the eighteenth-century audience filtered through the tears of their English counterparts without necessarily predicting their disillusioned ends. Clarissa had her antitypes, but the austere demands for virtue triumphant made by the critics, coupled with the popular desire for a happy ending, motivated the circumspect author to waft his heroine at last into the elysium her tears and trials deserved.

Sterne's view of sentiment was strictly esthetic and at times patronizing. He luxuriated in effusive displays of emotion; but, with the critical eye of an author objectively aware of his artistic self-indulgences, he sees the humor of his pathos: "[I] will introduce you among the rest to some tender-hearted damsel on whose cheek some bitter affliction has placed a tear, and having heard her story you shall take a white handkerchief from your pocket and wipe the moisture from her eyes and your own." [11] His ambivalence toward sentiment should not conceal the high regard he had for it. With Wordsworth, he could illustrate in his characters and their reactions to sentimental circumstance the thesis that one man is elevated above another in proportion to his ability to distinguish and respond to the pathetic and sublime in nature and humanity. But he did not care to emphasize, as Richardson did, the practical dangers that the sentimental character faced in his acutely sensitive progress through a world rarely attuned to his exquisite sensibility.

For convenience, then, we may distinguish a basically moral use of sentiment in Richardson from a basically esthetic view of it in Sterne. For later writers in the sentimental tradition this felt, if nowhere stipulated, distinction based criticisms of "excessive sensibility," of maudlin overreaction to a conceivably sentimental occasion, of callous pretenses at sentiment, of self-destructive displays of it in otherwise rational heroines. Both moral and esthetic responses to outer stimuli became rhetorical gestures in the later novels of sensibility which flooded the circulating libraries during the 1770's and 1780's—the decades between Walpole and Radcliffe. Whatever might have been genuine in Richardson's *Clarissa* and in Sterne's *The Sentimental Journey* became hackneyed matter for conditioned responses in the shopgirl whose bid for emotional respectability was made through the proxy of a victim or a heroine of sensibility. The same bourgeois sensibility that ran from prospect to prospect in search of the picturesque in nature indiscriminately worshiped these mass-produced graven images of ideal sentiment. To a modern audience, the better novels of the period merely epitomize the faults and pretensions of the worst.

The classic development of sensibility to either its absurd or tragic conclusion appears at the end of Henry Mackenzie's *The Man of Feeling* (1771), whose author is praised by Mrs. Reeve for being "moral, natural, and pathetic." Harley, the hero, has wept his way through a variety of sentimental circumstances in which he has fairly well established the relationship between spontaneous tears and benevolent actions. Like chivalric and sentimental heroes before and after him, he loves his lady fair in silence. As he lies dying of a fever complicated by a broken heart, she visits him to tell him of her love:

He seized her hand—a languid color reddened his cheek—a smile brightened faintly in his eye. As he gazed on her, it grew dim, it fixed, it closed—He sighed, and fell back on his seat—Miss Walton screamed at the sight—His aunt and the servants rushed into the room—they found them lying motionless together—His physician happened to call at that instant. Every art was tried to recover them—with Miss Walton they succeeded—But Harley was gone forever.[12]

Tragic irony such as this might be lost on the modern sensibility, but it continued to be emulated and to claim its tribute of at least a passing sigh through much of the 1790's. And it later exacted a like tribute when it appeared in the Victorian era in the sentimental realism of Charles Dickens.

Frances Sheridan's *The Memoirs of Miss Sidney Bidulph* (1761) is a classic as well as popular account of the pathetic trials of a young lady victimized not only by her sensibility but also by a nearly complete denial of natural inclination and free will. She remains duty bound first to a mother, then to a husband, and consistently restrains her feelings by "prudential motives." The male lead ultimately degenerates into weeping and raving, while Sidney herself outlines her calamity as a prelude to invoking her tears: "My heart is bursting—O Cecilia! What will become of my fond, my venerable parent, when she finds this daughter, this comfort of her old age . . . a poor abandoned outcast; lost to her husband's love, turned out of doors, despised, disgraced! my children too—I must leave them behind—My God, for what calamities hast thou ordained thy creature! Tears, tears, you may well flow." [13] The novel may still intrigue a reader whose sensibility is comprehensive enough to include *Clarissa* among its delights. Others may cynically construe, on esthetic principles, Johnson's compliment to Mrs. Sheridan when he questioned her right, on moral principles, "to make your readers suffer so much." [14]

Charlotte Smith was probably the best of the less famed among Mrs. Radcliffe's contemporaries. Like Ann Radcliffe, she did many things well—most of them better than Mrs. Radcliffe when they attempted to do the same thing. One reviewer admitted that he wept over *Celestina,* one of her early novels; another felt its sentiments dictated by "true sensibility." Since even as early as 1790 the reviewers had had their tear ducts very nearly drained by hordes of sentimental tales, the relatively consistent praise accorded Mrs. Smith indicates that she deserved the cant generalizations which flowed automatically from the reviewer's pen— "elevation of sentiment, a refinement of taste, a feeling, a delicacy" —all of which moved the affections and engaged the sympathy of the reader.[15]

Mrs. Smith was full of the zesty exuberance of emotional display which seemed to be requisite to an author who meant to exacerbate the bluntest as well as the most delicate of reader sensibilities. There are, along with the pages full of tears and occasional fainting fits, masculine versions of frustrated passion expressed in masochistic indulgences not available to or decorous for the heroine: "He felt for a moment disposed to dash himself against the wall, to tear his hair, to commit some of those wild and useless acts of desperation which intolerable and sudden anguish excites. . . ." [16] In this mood, beauty has power to momentarily soothe the self-destructive beast at large in the hero—"he cast his eyes on Althea, who, pale as ashes, sat like a figure of patient pity before him, and his fury for a moment subsided. . . ." He does, however, relapse. In *Celestina,* a male character does succeed in dashing his head against an iron grate until he loses consciousness and remains dormant for several days until saved from his madness by sweet human love. This variation on the sentimental is necessarily restricted to men and, in Mrs. Radcliffe, never receives the morbid emphasis the writers of the 1770's and 1780's placed on it. More Radcliffean is Orlando in Mrs. Smith's *The Old Manor House* who scratches his name on a covered seat in hopes that, should his love see it, it might "draw from her soft bosom one sigh more of tender recollection." [17]

For some commentators, the only major or nearly major novelist of the barren decades between Smollett and Austen was Fanny Burney. She represents a paradox of the times—a schizophrenic ability to see the gross exaggeration of feeling in sentimental rhetoric and yet to deal in it. When a hero imposes his whimsy and verbiage on Evelina, her artless common sense is offended; and she reacts accordingly: "But no! . . . It cannot be that you are so cruel! Softness itself is painted in your eyes.—You could not, surely, have the barbarity so wantonly to trifle with my misery." [18] "I turned away from this nonsense with real disgust," says Evelina; but her disgust did not prevent her author from relishing elsewhere a similar patter. A dialogue between hero and heroine need not be articulate in order to be touching:

"Angelic creature!" cried Delville, his own tears overflowing. . . .
"Ah, Delville!" cried she, a little reviving. . . .
"Too kind, too feeling Delville!" cried the penetrated Cecilia.[19]

The exaggeration is conventional and understood as such by readers who had been meeting with idealized love through a century of French heroic romance and sentimental drama. A significant happening in Burney's *The Wanderer* is a meeting between hero and heroine which is bathed in tears and, for the unsympathetic reader, in bathos as well: "so livid a paleness overspread her face, and so deadly a cold seemed to chill her blood, that, but for a friendly burst of tears, which ensued, her vital powers appeared to be threatened with immediate suspension." [20] Tears and sighs then choke the hero, rendering him speechless, while the young lady sympathizes but in silence: "I could not speak; I kissed his hand on my knee: and then, with yet more emotion, he again blessed me, and hurried out of the room.—leaving me almost drowned in tears . . ." (441).

The paradox of excessive sensibility was that it was a requisite expression of the beautiful soul, eighteenth-century style; but its appearance was often the cue for implicit or explicit censure of the young lady who indulged in it on the wrong occasions. A discriminating heroine not only distributed her tears lavishly but appropriately. The more common-sensical heroine—like Evelina—also knew how to react to the artificial rhetoric of sappy lovers whose style stemmed from the heroic rather than from the modern romance. In fact, the ability to discriminate between true and false sensibility becomes a moral as well as esthetic attribute for the more sophisticated sentimental heroine. But an ultimate judgment in certain cases is a subtle and perilous responsibility. Conflicts between nature and duty, as between emotion and reason, were aggravated by the tension between the inextricable strands of moral and esthetic sensibility variously motivating the heroine to action.

When, for example, the heroine of Miss Burney's *The Wanderer* is rescued from the clutches of a husband she had been forced to marry, her joy is almost immediately beguiled into despair when she "heard him called husband. . . .": "duty, for that horrible instant seemed in his favor; and had not Sir Jaspar called her by her maiden name, to attend to her own nearest relative, all her resistance had been subdued by an overwhelming dread that to resist might possibly be wrong" (V, 326). A wholesome consistency would doubtless have waived the question of duty in such a case. But the author's purpose is to thrill the reader with a last reminder of the heroine's *exquisite* sense of propriety even when it works at odds with the *common* sense of reason and morality.

The sentimental heroine is persistently and disinterestedly aware of the claims society might make on her. In most cases, moral and esthetic sensibility coalesce to one end—the supreme happiness of the heroine who is justly rewarded for the kind of disinterestedness illustrated in the following excerpt: "All is going well in Dame Fairfield's house, and any change in her situation will mean absolute peril for her, and yet she determines to let no personal consideration whatsoever interfere any longer with her causing an immediate investigation to be made into this fearful business" (*The Wanderer*, V, 7). The Radcliffean heroine consistently goes out of her way to involve herself in fearful and soul-shattering experiences when duty calls on her sensibility to renounce its relative tranquility for the higher purpose of ethical action.

The same ambivalence toward sentimentalizing appears in a rather remarkable anticipation of both the true and the parodied sentimental Gothic called *The Convent*; or, *The History of Sophia Nelson*, published in 1786 and ascribed to Anne Fuller. One young lady is characterized as having been educated by "her aunt of romantic memory": "She is as deeply read in romances, as her preceptress was, and squares her conduct exactly by their rules. Sometimes . . . she will deafen one with speeches of an hour long; her brother and sister she heartily despises, and comforts herself for her present mortification by the hope of one day discovering her true relations for whom she thinks, nay is certain, they have been exchanged." [21]

French heroic romances or fairy tales are the subject of the satire, but there is little difference between the turn it takes in *The Convent* and in Cherubina's effort in E. S. Barrett's *The Heroine* (1813) to provide herself with a father and background akin to those she had read of in the Gothic novels of the 1790's. In Mrs. Fuller's novel, false sentiment (particularly that species of it expressed by lovers full of freezing agues and burning fevers) is ridiculed and set off from Sternesque and Mackenzian sensibility, which is characterized by disinterested humanitarianism and nature appreciation. Enthusiasm in such cases is allowable, though a heroine does well to point out (or have pointed out for her) that she is not really inclined that way except under the stress of immediate (rather than fictional) inspiration. The convent itself eventually takes on an appropriately Gothic tone, with the Supérieure fulfilling her customary role as a heartless arbiter of the heroine's fate and an occasional motive for her tears, totterings, and climactic swoons.

While the moral strength of the heroine Sophia sets her off from the old romantic-chivalric breed of damsel-in-distress ("Time meliorated the violence of my grief into a calm and settled melancholy. . . . Yet notwithstanding my melancholy, my despair, I determined never to take the veil . . .") (II, 155), the letters exchanged between her and Edward, her beau, are altogether out of keeping with their sensible prose and dialogue elsewhere; indeed, they verge on unconscious parody of precisely the kind of exaggerated sentiment that they or their friends poke fun at in other contexts. Edward writes to Sophia in the convent:

O beloved of my soul! I come to rescue thee from thy oppressors! Say, wilt thou commit thyself to my care?—wilt thou accept my services? Heavens, what transport, that I who live but for thee, should be thy preserver. . . . I will free thee . . . or die. O life of my soul, I cannot exist without thee!—come to the arms of thy faithful lover; and that no vain scruples may prevent thee from making me happy, know that my uncle is dead, and that I inherit his whole fortune, which would prove a curse rather than a blessing, did I not cherish a hope of thy sharing it. (II, 203)

Possibly lovers are allowed these conventional extravagances on the Shakespearean hint that they share with poets and madmen a dispensation from the rhetorical limitations of the real language of men. Sophia, it should be noted, very often deviates into a refreshing directness of expression which intimates an impatience with her lover's stilted adventures in magniloquence: "No, my Lord, I have no scruples against being yours forever!—This is being tolerably explicit—but I have now no leisure for idle and fastidious refinements" (II, 203). Conceivably, Mrs. Fuller was quite aware of what she was doing in so deflating a hero's bombast. In any case, there is little difference between the satirical slash and innuendo here and in, say, Jane Austen's *Northanger Abbey*, except of course in the consummate degree of subtlety and ironic detachment which characterizes Austen's genius.

Despite a fairly successful Gothic scare or two toward the end, Maria Regina Roche's popular *The Children of the Abbey* (1796) is essentially a sentimental novel whose heroine sets the tone by "smiling through tears" and implying the moral sensibility that motivates them: "Sacred are such tears; they flow from the sweet source of social affection; the good alone can shed them." [22] But Mrs. Roche, like Mrs. Radcliffe, is critical of sentiment for its own sake. She indicates her moral bent when she introduces for implicit censure a fatuous young thing who "doats on sentimental correspondence."

While Amanda, the heroine, writes letters "blistered with tears," her moral rigor is exemplified in love scenes even more wooden than Mrs. Radcliffe's. The flawed hero suspects the heroine's virtue—a suspicion a Radcliffean hero could never entertain and preserve either his moral identity or esthetic value—and attempts to seduce her before he discovers his error in her indignant reaction and consequent admonition:

"Ah, my Lord, timely profit by mental correction, nor ever again encourage a passion which virtue cannot sanction, nor reason justify!"

—Thus spoke the angel:
And the grave rebuke, severe, to youthful beauty,
Added grave invincible. (30)

The formula writing continues to advance the usual moral exempla in dialogue that is only a shade removed from narrative editorializing: "I will not, from the thoughtlessness and impetuosity which lead so many of my sex astray, overstep the bounds of propriety, and to reinstate myself in the esteem of one person lose that of others, and, above all, that of my own heart" (200). Insofar as the novel was an instruction manual for young girls, the moral had to be—in the critic's favorite term—"unobjectionable." Innumerable meager and conventional plots were swathed in stereotyped moralizing whose only justification was the favorable critical reaction they would elicit from reviewers who could not extricate their esthetic evaluations from their ethical expectations.

When Amanda's father dies, the consequent flood of tears is as apt as the sentimental rhetoric that accompanies it. But to persevere overlong in grief, as Shakespeare's Claudius once pointed out to Hamlet, is both impious and self-indulgent. A disinterested moral consciousness characteristically asserts itself in tandem with an esthetic of grief which finally replaces its original chaos: "The turbulence of grief, and the agitation of suspense, gradually lessened in the mind of Amanda, and were succeeded by a soft and pleasing melancholy, which sprung from the consciousness of having always, to the best of her abilities, performed the duties imposed upon her, and supported her misfortunes with placid resignation" (222).

The "soft and pleasing melancholy," like the smiles which appear through tears, is the oxymoronic reminder of the contrasting tensions afflicting the heroine's sensibility and making absolute happiness impossible as well as gross. The one indestructible bit of egoism the heroine is obliged to possess is her sense of "conscious worth," which preserves her moral peace of mind whatever the chaos of circumstance and villainy do to disrupt its delicate esthetic balance. The height of moral sentimentalizing is generally reached when the heroine, like Amanda here, laments the passing of the villain, who, after compounding his villainies throughout the novel, dies abroad "without one connection, without one friend near him" (472). The intimated tear does him little good, but it could add considerably to the heroine's conscious worth, as it should add to her stature in the reader's eyes.

Sophia Lee's *The Recess* (1785), most relevant for its Gothic anticipations of the cave, the abbey, and the shadowy figures in

the garden, likewise imbues sensibility itself in macabre illumina-
tions. The heroine is grief-stricken when she thinks of her lover's
situation—and his concern about her. The reckoning up of conceivable fears and reasons to fear are clear anticipations of similar
passages in Mrs. Radcliffe: "Alas! I saw no more of my own fate,
than was inseparably interwoven with that of my lover. . . . Urged
by the generous excesses of which I knew his heart capable, he
has, for my sake, then, endangered his honour, liberty, and life." [23]
She then conceives of his possible death: "my wounded soul
shrunk from the bare idea—long faintings and delirium followed—
my fancy realized every image fraud had presented; I seemed to
behold every moment the chosen of my heart tried, sentenced,
executed; I drenched the maimed, yet beauteous form my soul for
ever worshipped in my tears, and hardly could be persuaded, during my lucid intervals, that Essex lived, and that his fate still
depended on my determination" (210).

It took no giant step to move from the overwrought figments of
the sentimental imagination to the illusory terrors plaguing Gothic
heroines. Increasingly, the terrors tend to justify the tears: "Sev-
ered thus from every tie both of nature and of choice, dead while
yet breathing, the deep melancholy which had seized upon my
brain soon tinctured my whole mass of blood; my intellect,
strangely blackened and confused, frequently realized scenes and
objects that never existed, annihilating many which daily passed
before my eyes" (211). Clearly the sensibility reacting to the following midnight garden scene is primed for ghostly visitations in
gloomy passageways: "The pale light served only to shadow out
his form—any human one must at such a moment have appalled
me. I shrieked and was half-fainting when the sound of his voice
dissipated my terror" (370).

III *The Sublime*

The doctrine of the sublime developed by eighteenth-century
psychological critics provided the Gothic novelist with an esthetic
alternative to mere beauty that eventually undermined the specious combination of sentiment and conventional morality which
had bemused critics and writers alike into believing that the novel
was a matter of tears and virtuous example. Sublimity was not
invented by Edmund Burke, nor did his *Philosophical Enquiry
into the Origin of our Ideas of the Sublime and Beautiful* (1757)

find its literate audience unprepared for a systematic account of a subject which had been current as a critical term since the late seventeenth century. The influential French critic Nicolas Boileau, decimated by John Keats for setting up a mechanical formula for the writing of poetry, proved the extent of his virtuosity and critical eclecticism by translating (and advocating as well) Longinus's rhetorical treatise *On the Sublime* (1674).

The early eighteenth-century critics were well aware that there were several graces beyond the reach of "art" in their restrictive and rule-ridden sense of the word. In England, they were uncomfortably aware of the giant Shakespeare forever illustrating the inadequacy of their critical recipes for artistic perfection; for he refused to abide either their questions or their answers. Longinus suggested a way out of the critical impasse they had made for themselves by providing a term and a predication which, though wonderfully vague, were thereby comprehensive enough to embody all the graces which could not be conveniently bundled into the concepts of art they codified and prescribed. "Sublimity," he said, "is the note which rings from a great mind." [24] It may be noted in passing that great minds do not dilute their greatness with tears except on great occasions; and their response to conventional moral codes tends to be ambiguous.

For Burke, the sublime was the supreme esthetic experience; and it was rooted in self-preservation, the primary law of human nature. Its basic ingredient was terror; its most powerful effect was astonishment, or "that state of the soul, in which all its motions are suspended, with some degree of horror." [25] The relevant attributes of the sublimely terrible are obscurity; power; privation ("Vacuity, Darkness, Solitude and Silence"); vastness; infinity (which "has a tendency to fill the mind with that sort of delightful horror, which is the most general effect, and truest test of the sublime"); succession and uniformity (the "artificial infinite"); difficulty ("When any work seems to have required immense force and labour to effect it, the idea is grand"); loudness (particularly when it comes suddenly in the midst of silence); and intermitting sounds, "low and tremulous" ("Now some low, confused, uncertain sounds, leave us in the same fearful anxiety concerning their causes, that no light, or an uncertain light does concerning the objects that surround us").

Burke's attributes are inductively derived from observation of nature, accounts of such observations, and from art. His esthetic is subjective and "sensational"—physiological. He is, of course, concerned with the psychological reaction which these attributes variously produce in a subject—"delightful horror" is his version of the distinction between terror and horror which Ann Radcliffe later makes. He likewise distinguishes between "pleasurable" reactions, which are positive esthetic responses to beauty, and "delightful" reactions, which, he stipulates, are negative esthetic responses to the sublime. The delightful are negative because the pain and terror associated with sublime feelings, objects, and incidents cannot produce any positive pleasure.

The intensity of the emotional reaction in the individual is the criterion of the degree of response he is capable of feeling and/or the object is capable of eliciting. Since self-preservation is the strongest source of emotion, the sublime feelings of terror and pain associated with it are the most intense—and, therefore, esthetically the most significant—experience an individual may undergo. The implicit paradox is that negative feelings are esthetically more fulfilling and appealing than positive ones. Beauty itself, which is merely a positive pleasure, loses its traditional status as the primary source of esthetic response because, in Burke's view, the principles by which it was traditionally judged are not confirmed by experience. Not proportion, not utility (certainly not morality), but relative intensity of response is the appropriate criterion of a beautiful as well as a sublime object. Since those attributes which Burke assigns the beautiful—smallness, smoothness, curvature, lightness, delicacy—cannot produce as intense a reaction as those associated with the sublime, the esthetic attraction of the beautiful is inevitably below that afforded by the sublime. Love and society are the congruent features of beauty which are respectively opposed to terror and self-preservation, the passion and major concern associated with the sublime. Burke is thereby enabled to conclude that the sublime and the beautiful are fundamentally opposed to each other because the first is rooted in pain and the second in pleasure. Nonetheless, since the painful feeling is more intense than the pleasurable one, sublime experiences are, from a purely esthetic point of view, more desirable than beautiful ones.

Whatever the limitations and perverse reasoning evident in Burke's esthetic, it was justified according to his premises and the empirical epistemology from which they were derived. In his introductory essay on taste, Burke assumes the Lockean position that all knowledge—including, of course, esthetic knowledge—stems from the senses. He argues that, since the sense world is the same for all of us and since our sense apparatus is fundamentally the same, it is reasonable to assume that our responses to that world are the same. If sameness thus functions at all levels of apprehension, it is likewise reasonable to infer that our imaginative, as well as our sensory, responses are the same. And if this is so, it is also true that there can be only one standard of taste. According to this standard of taste, one ascertainable class of attributes will produce sublime feelings in a representative observer; another set of attributes will produce "beautiful" feelings in the same observer. He is therefore justified in deriving the bipartite esthetic he goes on to develop. He realizes that variations in degree of esthetic response are inevitable because capacities and education vary; but, for individuals whose capacities and educations are the same, there is simply no disputing about taste—not because every man so organized and equipped is a sturdy individualist in his judgments but because every such man is inevitably determined toward the same judgment. When the Radcliffean heroine and her hero breathe like effusions to the natural decor around them they are illustrating, however unwittingly, Burke's thesis.

The final portion of Burke's *Enquiry* is concerned with the manner in which words affect the passions. He extends his primary attribute of the sublime, which is obscurity, to include verbal description. His famous coinage, "a clear idea is another name for a little idea," need not be read as a disdainful and perhaps superficial disparagement of clarity. It is more likely meant to distinguish words which appropriately retail consecutive thought, with minute attention to interlocking ideas, from the elaborate and suggestive imagery appropriate to art at its most sublime. Minute description in art or nature, he says, does not convey emotion nearly so well as obscure imagery highly charged with diction associated with greatness. The true purpose of descriptive writing is to excite in the reader emotions kindred to those which inspired the writer in the real or imagined presence of the subject he is writing about. Contrary to prescriptions for correct proportions, exact coloration, minuteness of detail, Burke advocates an art which will convey sublime feeling rather than beautiful imitation. "We yield to sympathy," he says, "what we refuse to description." [26] Sir Walter Scott rightly noted that a half-dozen painters would paint a half-dozen different versions of the castle of Udolpho because the imagery generally connotative of oppressive gloom and imminent terror does not convey an exact idea of the castle's façade and immediate locale. Burke provides the rationale of sublime effects which justifies Mrs. Radcliffe and strongly hints to the reader precisely how he is to piece out her imperfect description—not by idealizing a castle in the mind but rather by *feeling* the emotion implicit in the somber cast of the words.

Burke offered a convenient esthetic justification for a brand of novel that would incorporate and enlarge on the ghostly-ghastly elements of Elizabethan drama and the "graveyard" effusions that reveled in terror and obscurity for the sake of the emotional intensity these traditionally unartistic features of art produced. It is fairly clear that his version of the sublime was too limited to foster the variations on sublimity which appear in Mrs. Radcliffe's novels. A few writers before and after Burke filled in for his deficiencies by expanding the scope of the sublime to include moral and spiritual concepts which could not be easily inferred from an esthetic conceived in pain and brought forth as terror. The set pieces in Mrs. Radcliffe's novels (and in her biographical writings) transcend an esthetic of sheer terror for the moral assurance with which thoughts of God inspire her and her heroines.

IV   *The Picturesque*

Early eighteenth-century critics like Addison and John Dennis suggested the need for a systematic rationale of the sublime by their relatively inarticulate responses to scenes in nature which aroused their enthusiasm beyond the expressive limits of their esthetic vocabulary. Dennis uses a set of oxymorons to convey his reaction to an Alpine ascent of a perilous mountain path: "we walked upon the very brink, in a literal sense, of destruction; one Stumble and both life and carcass had been at once destroy'd. The sense of all this produc'd different motives in me, viz. a delightful horror, a terrible joy, and at the same time that I was infinitely pleas'd I trembled." [27] Anticipating Burke, Dennis relapses into the safety of contemporary personification to say of Nature, as of Shakespeare, "that her careless, irregular, and boldest strokes are her most admirable." He opposes this landscape to one which offers a "delight consistent with Reason"—full of "flowery meads and murmuring streams."

The two views of nature which parallel the dreadfully sublime and the tepidly beautiful in Burke parallel also the landscape painters who represented to the great majority of Englishmen all of the Alpine sublimity and beauty they were likely to see. Salvator Rosa (1615–73) and Claude Lorrain (1600–82), along with Nicolas Poussin (1594–1665), prepared the English audience for the verbal renditions of Italian and Provençal landscapes which either relieve or intensify the Gothic horrors with which the Radcliffean heroine is customarily surrounded. Rosa's sublime was filled with impending mountains, darksome caves, barren crags, savage wildernesses, gloomy skies, blasted trees, and, appropriately to humanize a tempestuous scene, frequent adumbrations of somber figures barely recognizable as banditti or *Walpurgisnacht* revelers. "Dreamy sweetness" was the contrasted character of Claude's idyllic landscapes which depicted a timeless pastoral scene where eternal springtime decked out the rolling lawns and embowering trees surrounding the dabbed-in figures of shepherds and their flocks. Poussin's effects were somewhere intermediate between these extremes, with perhaps more Claude than Rosa in his characteristically "noble" landscapes.

The English audience received its Italian landscaping through print facsimiles which, according to Shaftesbury, were the greatest invention since printing. By the middle of the century all men of taste collected them; they became conversation pieces and subjects of social exchange and debate. While Samuel Johnson said he could never suspend his disbelief long enough to visualize an actual landscape from a print, his friend Sir John Hawkins expressed the common viewer's facility at doing so when he said that prints "presented to my mind the objects themselves and . . . my imagination realized the prospect before me." Hours were spent poring over prints, as if they were books; and the result was that the connoisseur—who was simply the man of sensibility in a different nomenclature—began to see the English countryside imbued with Italian light.

A mechanical aid to this beautiful deception was the "Claude glass," through which a viewer could see the relative glare of a local propsect softened by the mellowing shades of a Claudean landscape. More lasting effects were secured by the "improvers," landscape architects like Lancelot "Capability" Brown whose armed vision quickly discerned the potential of a wealthy landowner's estate to emulate the condition of art. River courses were changed, groves removed or transplanted, perspectives added or subtracted, even artifacts like Gothic ruins and hermits' caves were added to a landscape in order to make it more effectively represent the painting it was virtually based upon. Controversies accordingly raged over the just proportion of art to nature which a landscape should possess. The late eighteenth-century reviewers commented on and conveyed the subtle or gross differences between men like Brown, Richard Payne Knight, Uvedale Price, and Humphrey Repton concerning the merits of turning nature into art. The result of both practice and controversy was that very few, even among the fair readers who were to support the Gothic novel, were unaware of the "picturesque" in nature as a vital esthetic concern.

The degree of perfection attained by poetry and painting is, according to one early eighteenth-century writer, directly proportional to their reciprocal emulations: "The nearer the Poet approaches to the Painter, the more perfect he is; and the more perfect the Painter, the more he imitates the Poet." [28] *The Critical Review* comments on John Dyer's poem "The Fleece" as if it were a painting: "In this agreeable landscape we perceive that the objects are properly placed, the figures well grouped, and the ordonnance of the piece just and natural. The colors are excellent, the strokes masterly, and the whole picture highly finished." [29] James Thomson is used as a kind of critique on Rosa, partly, we may infer, because, as George Keate wrote, the poet could deepen the psychological contours barely suggested in the painter's art by "unveil[ing] external appearances and paint[ing] that precious disposition of mind which fixed them." [30] Thomson's *Seasons* were themselves used by one connoisseur to instruct his son in the art of painting. With Salvator highlighting his "Winter" and Claude imbuing his "Summer," Thomson had only to join the two with a "Spring" full of Poussin to set himself down as an archtranslator into verse of "Whate'er Lorrain light-touched with softening Hue,/ Or savage Rosa dash'd, or learned Poussin drew."

Joseph Warton admitted that Thomson's *Seasons* were "very instrumental in diffusing a general taste for the beauties of nature and landscape." [31] Warton also extended his synesthesia of artistic interchange by crediting Capability Brown with having converted back into their natural setting Thomson's verbal transcriptions of Rosa, Lorrain, and Poussin. Elizabeth Montagu called Brown a "great poet," thereby admitting the success of his self-professed emulation of "sweet pastorals and elegiacs" in his gardening art. There is a complimentary turn to the light satire embroidering the wish of a man who hoped to die before Brown so that he might get to heaven before Brown improved it.

Thomas Green's avid appreciation of Mrs. Radcliffe's nature settings—unlike some of the reviewers of her novels, his taste for her description was insatiable—was anticipated by Mrs. Montagu who felt that the scenery embellishing a novel was esthetically more interesting than the story it told. The peculiar advantage the writer had over the painter was that he could combine all styles in one, fusing the somber landscapes of Rosa with the pale cast of a Claudean summer. Anna Seward offers a guide for the reading of scenic descriptions which the modern reader may find particularly solacing when faced with the leisurely expanse of a Radcliffean canvas as it unfolds through interminable pages: "We should look attentatively at this landscape, but not consider them for a longer time than we could, without weariness, gaze at a landscape of Claude's or Salvator's." [32] Her advice recalls Burke's impatience with those who feel that scenic description should strive for laboriously detailed imitation rather than for emotionally suggestive impression.

Burke's correlative emphasis on obscurity as the primary attribute of the sublime was confirmed not only by the overall vagueness of landscape painting, whether in Rosa or Lorrain, but also by the careless brushstrokes which went into the making of its human figures and the "groupings" they composed. At times delegating to an apprentice the task of blotting in a requisite figure or group, the painters likewise offered an additional precedent outside sentimental tradition for writers who used their characters as mediums through which the reader experienced the beautiful and sublime in word, deed, and scenic decor. If a Radcliffean heroine seems to lose whatever individuality she hinted at when fleeing amid mountains and cataracts, she is simply establishing her representative identity with the bits and dashes of humanity adding a moral interest to a Salvatorean setting. The nod in the direction of contemporary prints was not lost on the cultured contemporary reader. Like Claude, the landscaping novelist "sinks partial form in general effect" until his characters seem, like Salvator's, "little groups of figures dropped from a whirlwind." [33]

The Deistic tendency, which spiritualized the sublime through terror and up to God, moralized as well the irregular and wild effects of Salvator, who was (the painter John Constable said) "a great favorite with novel writers, particularly the ladies." Lady Morgan, one of the ladies, found his landscapes "pregnant with moral interest, and calculated to awaken the human sympathies. . . . The wayworn traveller, the benighted pilgrim, the shipwrecked mariner . . . become images that engage the heart as well as the eye, and give to the inanimate character of landscape a moral action. . . ." [34] Another commentator notes that the figures are introduced precisely so that they can aid us to "employ our reflections." In fact, the paintings were customarily "read" as if they were books.

Reciprocally, when a Radcliffean heroine moralized over nature she was eliciting a reader response kindred to that elicited by landscape prints. A painting described for its Gothic habiliments echoes the "Graveyard" poets and anticipates La Motte's *sic transit* reflections in *The Romance of the Forest*: "ruins of castles, palaces, temples, and deserted religious houses . . . whatever else may serve the debility, the disappointments, and the dissolution of humanity; which, by cooperating with the dreary aspect of autumnal nature . . . fill the mind with melancholy and incline it to serious reflections." [35] The spiritual qualities of nature are ritualistically inferred from both paintings and landscapes, whose ends are to "lead the intellectual Mind to . . . admire Perfection infinite —/ Heavens matchless Skill, Benevolence, and Pow'r." [36]

Elizabeth Carter directly anticipates the Radcliffean heroine when she notes that "sublime views of wild uncultivated nature," whether in nature or in Salvator, caused "the soul to expand itself and feel at once the greatness of its capacities and the littleness of its pursuits." [37] In sum, the eighteenth-century readers were conditioned to expect certain reactions and moods occasioned in a sensitive heroine by particular scenic descriptions. By legitimate extension, they were themselves conditioned to respond through a heroine to the natural scene they vicariously shared.

The "picturesque" itself was particularly well adapted to verbal transcription because it was essentially a blend of the sublime and the beautiful which was not often found in nature and hardly at all in the two favorite landscape painters. Uvedale Price pointed up the valuable esthetic effect occasioned by looking first at a Rosa, then at a Lorrain. "Contrast," which is a comprehensive narrative as well as pictorial technique in Mrs. Radcliffe, not only provided the viewer with a full range of esthetic experience but also intensified the beautiful by opposing it to the sublime and further exalting the sublime against the modifying tones of the beautiful. While Burke had spoken against the indiscriminate combination of the two, the positive effect each had on the other in verbal redactions of the picturesque transcended his objections —at least for the synthesizing imaginations of the conditioned reader.

But the Gothic novel of the 1790's incorporated the last flowering of the picturesque as it did of the sentimental. If, as some commentators suppose, Mrs. Radcliffe's major contribution to the novel was her lavish nature descriptions, it was a contribution that was soon exhausted, at least in the manner and spirit with which she rendered it. The conventional moralizing, the sentimental redundancies, the mechanical juxtaposition of the sublime and the beautiful, the consequent apostrophes to God—all these required the kind of transvaluation into the authentic individual communion with nature which the Romantic poets were soon to provide. Barrett's *The Heroine* contains a salutary parody of the kind of Radcliffean sentiment and situation which helped render the picturesque a tedious affectation: "There is a lady in the *Romance of the Highlands* who . . . when dying, and . . . about to disclose the circumstances of a horrid murder . . . unfortunately expended her last breath in a beautiful description of the verdant hills, rising sun, all nature smiling, and a few streaks of purple in the east." [38]

Much later, in his *The Guide to the Lakes*, William Wordsworth defined his organic conception of the sublime and the beautiful in a synthesis which resolved Burke's arbitrary division beyond the insubstantial and poorly defined combinations attempted by the cult of the picturesque: "Sublimity is the result of Nature's first dealings with the superficies of the earth; but the general tendency of her subsequent operations is towards the production of beauty;

by a multiplicity of symmetrical parts uniting in a consistent whole." [39]

Burke's esthetic of terror provided a rationale for an emergent literature of the supernatural which had remained only potential or subsidiary until Walpole. By locating his supreme esthetic in an intense and admittedly negative emotional response he also suggested an available means whereby sheer sensationalism could gain respectibility and human interest. The novel of sensibility doted on the emotional displays of hypersensitive heroines whose characteristic attitude was a swoon prefaced by tears. The indicated recipe was simple: abstract one of these heroines from her stereotyped domestic turmoils and place her, with her sensibilities fully primed, in the midst of terrors which would demonstrably agitate the hearts and imaginations of strong men. If, as Burke said, self-preservation was the basis for the sublimest esthetic experience; if terror was the most exciting emotion a human might undergo; if a sense of absolute power directing these terrors from somewhere in the infinite obscure was felt as the prime threat to the self struggling for preservation—then a fragile vessel of femininity, aghast at a harsh word or social solecism, was an ideal medium for vicarious terror. When placed amid a congeries of hyperbolic and continuing threats to her existence from a source all-powerful, always obscured, and certainly unnatural, if not diabolically supernatural, her fragility, fears, and ideal stature were reciprocally heightened.

In the long run, the union between an amoral esthetic and a conventional ethic was too specious and unnatural to last. "Monk" Lewis would compound and reify the terror, ignore the sentimental, and use his supernatural effects for descents into diabolism. Studied flights through nature to God would lose their conventional status as literary set pieces when Wordsworth actually lived what Ann Radcliffe wrote into her heroine's rhapsodizings. But, during the 1790's, the Radcliffean synthesis of sentiment and terror seemed the culminating synthesis of esthetic prescript and literary practice which an emergent Romanticism had more or less unwittingly been struggling to effect.

CHAPTER 3

The Castles of Athlin and Dunbayne

*T*HE *Castles of Athlin and Dunbayne* (1789) is Ann Radcliffe's tentative and not very successful first effort at joining modern with medieval romance in the manner suggested by Walpole and better illustrated by Clara Reeve. There is none of the absolute extravagance of Walpole's sensationalism, but there is plenty of pseudoknightly adventure spiced with a suggestive smattering of eighteenth-century sentimentality. The work is short —a novelette rather than a novel—the characterization is trite and often abortive; the plot, disconnected; and the action, sufficiently unmotivated either by character or circumstance to verge not only on the incredible but too often on the ridiculous. It has the usual significance of a mediocre first novel by a maturing talent: it demonstrates the general bent of the author's developing powers while indicating to the critic's retrospective view precisely what the author thought worth retaining and expanding in her later works and what she wisely discarded.

I *Summary*

The setting is the northeast coast of the Scottish Highlands toward the end of the sixteenth century. Previous to the action of the novel, the former Earl of Athlin had been ensnared and slain through the wiles of the villain of the piece, Malcolm, Baron of the neighboring castle of Dunbayne. The novel opens with the coming of age of the Earl's son, Osbert, who seeks vengeance for his father's murder by attempting a sneak attack on Dunbayne with a small band of loyal followers. These followers include preeminently the secondary but more engaging hero of the novel, Alleyn, a peasant with significantly noble attributes whom Osbert had met while wandering lost in the forest. Alleyn had almost immediately characterized himself as an enemy to Malcolm and is therefore a friend to virtue, but nothing is said on either side that accounts for "the whole truth flashing on his mind" that Osbert was the son of the lord "whom he had been taught to love." Alleyn forthwith pledges his fidelity and aid to Osbert, guides him back to Athlin, and stays to participate—in the medieval guise of the stranger-knight—in the jousting games where he inevitably "bears off each prize of chivalry."

In spite of Alleyn's aid, the attack on Malcolm's castle is frustrated, and both he and Osbert are captured. The diabolical Baron refuses to accept ransom for his prisoners and demands instead Osbert's young and beautiful sister Mary in exchange for Osbert's life. Mary herself is soon captured by a band of armed men, borne to a "horrible cave," where she faints and awakens to find—Alleyn, who had managed to escape from the Baron's clutches. Alleyn's rather lengthy account of his escape is told in the presence of Mary and her (and Osbert's) mother, Matilda, who is alarmed at her daughter's fainting at the conclusion of Alleyn's narrative—not so much because of the physical distress it indicates but because of the emotional condition she feels it illustrates. Mary's Desdemona-like sympathy with Alleyn's trials suggests she is in love with him. Since marriage with a peasant, however praiseworthy he may be, is out of the question for Mary, thoughts of love should likewise be wiped from her mind.

Meanwhile, Osbert at Dunbayne is suffering both the petty villainies of Malcolm and the more distressing psychological pains caused by his disinterested concern with the emotional and mental reaction to his imprisonment that his family and friends must themselves be suffering. This psychological distress is compounded by his seeing and finally gaining access to the imprisoned mother and daughter of the former Baron of Dunbayne, the brother of Malcolm, who have been wrongfully deprived of their freedom and properties for some fifteen years, or from a time soon after the Baroness had left her native Switzerland to come to Scotland with her husband. He had died not long after their arrival, leaving her and her two children (a son has supposedly died in childhood) at the mercy of the usurping Malcolm. Osbert's initial compassion for the two ladies quickly deepens to love for the daughter. Alleyn soon relieves Matilda from the necessity of choosing between her son's life and her daughter's virtue by rescuing Osbert, who regrets that he must leave the daughter, Laura, behind with only the promise that he will do all in his power to effect her escape. Soon after Osbert's rescue, a shipwreck brings under his protection a Swiss stranger who turns out to be a relative of the imprisoned Baroness. The stranger—Count de Santmorin—soon falls in love with Mary, his suit is favored by both Matilda and Osbert, while Alleyn's precipitate avowal of love to Mary herself gains him her temporary disdain, and he soon after disappears from the castle.

The novel concludes with a jumble of events and revelations which haphazardly bring about the dénouement we have been expecting for some time now, though the author manages to spring at least one surprise on us before fulfilling our expectations. Malcolm attacks Athlin, is defeated, and confesses on his deathbed both his sins in general and the specific and significant fact that he had given the Baroness's son to a peasant couple who have since disappeared. Osbert, stabbed in a ruined part of his own castle, recovers in time for an intended wedding with Laura, which, however, is postponed when Mary is again spirited away by a band of armed men. Since Malcolm is dead, a villain seems wanting as perpetrator of this act, nor has there been anything in the characterization so far to indicate that it might be the actual culprit, Count de Santmorin, whose suit had been rejected by Mary. The Count is unmasked when Alleyn rescues Mary; and, though clearly contrite over his momentary lapse from virtue, Santmorin is confessedly guilty of surrendering to a passion that had made him directly responsible for Mary's abduction and indirectly the cause of Osbert's near assassination. Though class prejudice still holds sway in the minds of Osbert and Matilda, the revelation of Alleyn as the long-lost son of the Baroness fortunately resolves a dilemma and allows Mary to wed the man she loves and to retain the class status her family insists upon. Osbert and Laura will also marry.

The moral tag concluding the novel emphasizes the role divine justice plays in shaping the destiny of men according to its inscrutable and beneficent wisdom: "It is now seen that those virtues which stimulated him [Alleyn] to prosecute for another the cause of justice, mysteriously urged him to the recovery of his rights. Virtue may for a time be pursued by misfortune,—and justice be obscured by the transient triumphs of vice; but the Power whose peculiar attributes they are, clears away the clouds of error, and even in this world establishes his THRONE OF JUSTICE" (764). However forced the moral conclusion might seem, it clearly justifies the instructional value of the novel and, in so doing, anticipates comparable conclusions to the rest of Ann Radcliffe's novels. The prime virtue, which is portrayed in Alleyn most of all (but present in all characters insofar as they are virtuous), is disinterestedness, or a selfless concern for the good of others. And this virtue Mrs. Radcliffe impresses on her readers with redundant exemplification in her later novels.

II *Esthetic Morality*

Disinterestedness here and always is in Mrs. Radcliffe's view an esthetic and ethically attractive force in the dramatic interplay of characters. The unspoken bond between a hero and heroine is their mutual concern with each other in spite of the personal trials each inevitably undergoes. The exquisitely virtuous sensibility of Osbert is defined by his generous capacity to forget his own distress as a prisoner condemned to death. His solace in misery is that adversity has at any rate conditioned him to sympathize with others by developing his innate capacity for disinterestedness. His clanking medieval antecedents show through his sentimental vesture when his indignation at the sight of the imprisoned ladies (Laura and her mother) inspires him with a longing "to become at once the champion of virtue and the deliverer of oppressed innocence." He is hardly concerned when he is told a bit later that he will die the next day, but he is inexpressibly delighted to know that Alleyn has escaped. When the sadistic Baron leads Osbert out to a mock-execution, he gains no little satisfaction from his prisoner's swoon. As a villain incapable of understanding disinterested motives or noble feeling, Malcolm has mistakenly supposed that terror in the face of death was the cause of his victim's fainting fit. In psychological fact, it was pity for his mother's anticipated grief that had brought it on.

The diluted and infrequent presentation of Laura prevents her from illustrating as profusely as later Radcliffean heroines do the disinterestedness that would make her a fit mate for Osbert. But these heroines are, by and large, interchangeable so far as this primary virtue is concerned. Mary's disinterestedness establishes her as the moral ideal which the feminine lead invariably holds in the Radcliffean ethic. Her dilemma is doubtless derived from Shakespeare's *Measure for Measure*, though her decision to sacrifice herself to Malcolm's lust and vengeance in order to save her

brother renders her morally superior to Shakespeare's heroine—
at least according to sentimental standards of morality—while calling attention to her relatively dehumanized, semiallegorical character.

She makes this decision privately, thereby bearing its horrible
implications alone and without the cathartic relief she would
receive by telling her mother what she intended to do. Silence in
grief and under duress is a prerogative assigned to the Radcliffean
heroine in order to increase her psychological sufferings and consequently her moral stature. Not only does Mary conceal her
decision and the dread she feels at her prospects, but she also does
what she can to solace her mother, who imagines that the decision
is hers to make. An added fillip is rather caustically applied to
Mary's already aggravated emotional state when she is forced to
struggle against her love for Alleyn. Her moral and social responsibility to her family requires that she marry for their interest
rather than for her own. But except to an audience duly conditioned for tears by much exposure to sentimental literature, Mary's
disinterested suffering consistently fails to elicit the compassion
Mrs. Radcliffe is so clearly calling for.

Disinterestedness implies a control over passion which the Radcliffean heroine almost always possesses—except when, in private,
she gives way to the tears that her distresses entitle her to. She
never speaks her love; she barely reveals "the secret that trembles
on her lips" through "the soft timidity of her eye, and the tender
glow of her cheek." When the hero precipitously avows his love,
either through speech or gesture, the heroine responds with a sense
of offended virtue, though her natural feelings—or a significant
part of them—are on the side of the offender. Caught off guard by
the sudden apparition of his loved one as he stands contemplating
her picture, Alleyn spontaneously kisses—her hand: "His tongue
would have told her that he loved; but his emotion and the repulsive look of Mary prevented him. She instantly disengaged
herself with an air of offended dignity, and casting on him a look
of mingled anger and concern, withdrew in silence" (750).

Even when Alleyn's birth has been proved equal to his merit,
Mary remains to the end tongue-tied by a reserve that signifies the
decorous refinement of her sensibility: "A smile of ineffable sweetness broke through the melancholy which had long clouded her
features, and which even the present discovery had not been able

entirely to dissipate, and her eye gave the consent which her tongue refused to utter" (763). Not only is the assent of the eye the sufficient and appropriate sign of the heroine's sensibility, but it is also her gracious recognition of a like sensibility in the hero's emotional makeup. The inner ear of an adequate hero is necessarily attuned to the discourse of the eye. Words, in such a case, would not only be redundant but in bad taste.

Mrs. Radcliffe's initial description of Osbert anticipates in its general and rather vacuous use of complimentary phrase and adjective similar descriptions in her later novels: "nature had given him a mind ardent and susceptible, to which education had added refinement and expansion. The visions of genius were bright in his imagination, and his heart, unchilled by the touch of disappointment, glowed with all the warmth of benevolence" (721). This kind of description is rhetorical rather than dramatic: the conventional flow of words defining the typical hero run mechanically from the author's pen. They do not develop organically from any specific idea of genius or benevolence conceived by her own imaginative powers. In practice, this ardent and susceptible mind responds vitally to art and nature alike—esthetic responses that also indicate his ethical stance. Osbert, like Ann Radcliffe and most of her later heroes and heroines, "delighted in the terrible and in the grand, more than in the softer landscape." But the attenuated version of the sublime that he wanders through is found in the paintings of Salvator Rosa rather than in the Scottish Highlands.

III *The Heroine*

The heroines, who play a relatively small role in this first novel, are if anything even less particularized, though the generalized contours of the later Radcliffean heroines can be seen barely emerging in the seventeen-year-old Mary. She "had the accomplishments of riper years, with the touching simplicity of youth," while the "graces of her person were inferior only to those of her mind, which illumined her countenance with inimitable expression." In later characterization there is evidence that the stereotyped sentimental heroine would provide Mrs. Radcliffe with the emotional barometer for measuring the sometimes subtle changes in the atmosphere of terror and moral deviation which permeated her works: "Nature had bestowed on her a heart susceptible of all the fine emotions of delicate passion; a heart which vibrated in unison with the sweetest feelings of humanity; a mind, quick in perceiving the nicest lines of moral rectitude, and strenuous to act up to its perceptions" (737). And, the author significantly notes, while such powers of discrimination were hardly necessary to suffer in the midst of her present terrors (which even a common mind would have found intolerable), they nonetheless "served . . . to sharpen the points of affliction, to increase their force, and to disclose in stronger light the various horrors of her situation."

Such a generalized account hardly compensates for the dearth of dramatic confrontation and detail necessary to activate and prove the heroine's susceptibility to her afflictions and horrors; it has, at best, the conventional appeal of the commonplace, which need only make a rhetorical gesture in the general direction of an action or characterization. The well-conditioned reader then provides the appropriate detail that his imagination has been stocked with by previous encounters with like actions and characters in novels and dramatic works that are only nominally different from the one now being read.

Since Ann Radcliffe persistently balks at any detailed description of any actual physical violence, the morbid projections of the heroine made her a necessary as well as an ideal medium for a congeries of alternative horrors that are terrifically enhanced to the reader because they take place in the mind of a highly sensitized reagent: "Here she beheld herself entombed in the arms of the murderer;—there, the spectacle of her beloved brother, encircled with chains, and awaiting the stroke of death arose to her imagination . . . fancy gave her the horrors of reality. . . . [only] by obliterating from her memory the image of virtue, could [she have] a chance of obtaining a horrid tranquillity" (737). In a later reduction of disinterestedness to its dismal conclusion, she decides on this horrid tranquillity from among "the dreadful choice of horrors" by nobly resigning herself to the Baron.

If the virtue underlying misery is that it teaches a given hero to sympathize with the woes of others, the superficial virtue of melancholy for heroines is the cosmetic effect it has on their already beautiful features: "Sorrow and interesting langour" added to Mary's appearance a dimension beyond the reach of mere healthy loveliness. The implication is that this evidence of grief amid the contrasting features of beauty is an outer sign of some inner soul-stretching occasioned by trials faced and horrors endured. The mellowing of grief at her husband's death eventually produced a melancholy in Matilda that "gave a soft and interesting shade to the natural dignity of her character."

Matilda suffers what is surely the most egregious moral dilemma of the novel, though our own vicarious suffering is very much alleviated by the apathetic and barely delineated character of the tormented mother.

The critical situation of Matilda can scarcely be imagined in its full extent. Torn by the conflict of opposite interest, her brain was the seat of tumult and wild dismay. Whichever way she looked, destruction closed the view. The murderer of the husband now sought to murder the happiness of the daughter. On the sentence of the mother hung the final fate of the son. In rejecting these terms, she would give him instant death; in accepting them, her conduct would be repugnant to the feelings of indignant virtue, and to the tender injured memory of her murdered lord. . . . Honour, humanity, parental tenderness, bade her save her son; yet by a strange contrariety of interests, the same virtues pleaded with a voice equally powerful for the reverse of the sentence. Hitherto hope had still illumined her mind with a distant ray; she now found herself in the darkness of despair, whose glooms were interrupted only by the gleams of horror which arose from the altar on which was to be sacrificed one of her beloved children. (736)

A sign of vintage Radcliffe is this ability to extract the last bitter measure of conflicting sensation from the ethical cul-de-sac in which she places Matilda. Similar paragraphs full of alternative evils dot her later work; at their best, they give some substance and intensity to rhetorical patterns of emotional expression that she inherited from her sentimental sources. By piling moral paradoxes on horrible alternative, Mrs. Radcliffe achieves a highly dramatic effect through the collectivity when it is bundled into a small space and focused on the imagination of the sympathetic reader.

IV   *The Villain*

The bare outlines of full-fledged villains like Montoni or Schedoni clearly stand out in the strongly, if sketchily, drawn character of Malcolm. His precedents in literature are probably the vice figure and ogre rather than, say, Iago, though he does share with

Shakespeare's archvillain that dehumanized evil that Coleridge called "motiveless malignity." He also shares with later Radcliffean villains generic characteristics which are simply listed rather than dramatically portrayed: he is ambitious, "proud, oppressive, revengeful," his mind "haughty and unaccustomed to control," though cowardice is typically "unknown to him." Since the heroine is the incarnation of disinterestedness, the villain is the embodiment of self-interest. While Malcolm is no dialectician, later villains (Montalt and Montoni) share with Milton's Satan a rhetorical facility at equivocating with words like "nature" and "necessity" to prove that their evil is really good, or, at any rate, expedient. Malcolm's pretensions to satanic majesty are limited to dire intimations—"I go to meditate on your destiny"—which inspire no one, the reader least of all, with any fear.

But Malcolm's diabolical concepts of psychological suffering are, if anything, more subtle and morbid than those hinted at or executed by his Radcliffean successors. Like all villains, he is a prey to his uncontrollable passions; they never allow him to act with consistency, "but, torn by conflicting energies, the gratification of one propensity is destruction to the enjoyment of another." Malcolm consequently refuses to accept ransom for the captured Oswald because his desire for revenge overcomes his avarice; but, since he also lusts after Mary, he must forgo revenge in order to gain her. His passions obscure his sense of values at one point when he deviates into an act of apparent mercy by reprieving some inefficient sentinels from death because of his exuberant joy at the thought of executing Oswald. He then recollects that he must forgo that pleasure too if he is to have Mary. The villain suffers his immoral dilemmas. Malcolm's rather meager solace amid a turmoil of conflicting passions derives from the suspense with which he torments Oswald before regretfully reprieving him at the last moment.

Before Malcolm comes to the miserable end that his acts and passions predict for him, he gains an insight into his own evil ingenuity whereby he perceives that, all unwittingly, he had really been working out an ideal revenge by fulfilling his lust. Osbert will suffer an anguish in life far greater than death alone could inflict since he will live knowing that his sister's honor and his mother's piece of mind have been the price of his freedom: "[Malcolm] was surprised that his invention had not before supplied him with this means of torture; for the first time he wel-comed love as the instrument of his revenge; and the charms of Mary were heightened by the ardent colours of his passion" (738). Possibly because Mrs. Radcliffe realized that the insistent deca-dence of her villain's morbid calculations kept him from achieving a credible human dimension, she did not allow the evil resolution of her later villains to stand unqualified by some humanizing dia-logue or sentiment. Mrs. Radcliffe decorously and shrewdly ex-changed the villain's perspective on his thoughts and possible acts for the heroine's. The fear-ridden sensibilities of an Emily expand the villain's capacity for evil far beyond the limits of his relatively meager imagination.

Malcolm's contrived and melodramatic deathbed contrition, with its conventional piety and gratuitous epitaph ("Thus termi-nated the life of a man whose understanding might have reached the happiness of virtue"), emphasizes his allegorical character by attenuating whatever consistency his previous portrayal had devel-oped. (Mrs. Radcliffe would never allow her villains to die with-out confessing an awareness of their errors.) But his death is in all ways anticlimactic. He had already been long lost in Mrs. Rad-cliffe's unwieldy shuffling of the narrative sequences consequent on the appearance of the "mixed" character, de Santmorin.

V   Technique and Structure

Since there is no plot to speak of, there are no narrative com-plexities to comment on. The action is developed in a series of vignettes arbitrarily and sometimes irritatingly pasted together. There are Gothic incidents amid the Gothic surroundings of castle, dungeon, and subterraneous passageways—there are even instant *expliqués* of apparent supernatural phenomena. But, as with the abortive apostrophes to natural beauty or sublimity, they are worth noting only because, in rudimentary form, they illustrate Mrs. Radcliffe's tentative and clumsy apprentice efforts with the tools of her trade. Certain motifs out of fairy lore, chivalric tale, or Walpole appear to expand a vignette or pretend to a dramatic effect: the peasant-prince, the strawberry mark, recalcitrant locks, secret panels, the room in which the heroine is kept or to which she retreats, garrulous servants, love-longing. With varying em-phasis, many of these features reappear in the later novels as sounding boards for sensibility and motives for terror or suspense.

Since Mrs. Radcliffe was neither interested in nor capable of enlivening dramatic narrative of the old romantic variety, she dropped the chivalric emphasis, allowing sieges, pitched battles, forays, and frays to stand as obscure portions of the masculine-world background which only now and then impinged on her heroine's terror-ridden sensibility. The change in emphasis is a consequence of a changed perspective. Until Vivaldi (in *The Italian*), the heroine, not the hero, mediates the Radcliffean chamber of horrors to the susceptible reader. Since she could not retail furious outer action piping hot to an expectant audience, she fell back on the inner drama of sensibility derived from the modern novel. And manly fortitude lacks the vacillation and range of feminine sensibility which is by nature and conditioning ideally susceptible to the thrilling variations counterpointing the theme of horror which grounds Radcliffean Gothic.

Unless a reader musters some sympathy for Mary and Matilda, there is no suspense in the novel that is not the result of bad organization or dramatic ineptness. The emphasis on masculine fast-action, the little time alloted to description, the relatively few probes of dire alternatives, along with an abundance of rhetorical faults, keep the reader's mind comfortably disengaged from the tensions that a hero or heroine is professedly suffering. There are a few crude attempts at holding off a dire dénouement—the "inflexible silence" of the villain and the interpolated tale. Both are used with some subtlety for suspenseful effects in later novels, but Mrs. Radcliffe never used the interpolated tale with the abandon which characterized her imitators and the German horror novelists.

Possibly the best bit of suspense in *Castles* was adventitious, a consequence of dramatic slovenliness rather than of strength. We are truly mystified when Mary is spirited away for the second time, just as we are by Osbert's stabbing. With the Baron dead, there is no villain on the scene; and we have enough faith in the author's dramatic integrity to suppose she will not introduce a new character simply to forestall for a while the end of this all-too-short novelette. When the Count is unveiled as the culprit, we can see in retrospect that, given the sentimental conventions bracing his character, his emotion was strong enough for him to conspire against the peace of the Athlin household. We may wonder whether Mrs. Radcliffe saw that in advance of writing it out; however, the fumbling disposition of the narrative generally may keep us from crediting her with any preconceived ingenuity.

Matters of structure and style are worth dealing with in a concluding appraisal of this barely mediocre novel not simply because they illustrate the degree of necessary improvement in store for Mrs. Radcliffe. They also illustrate deficiencies which continued to mark the great majority of Gothic novels from the 1790's through the middle of the following century. The reason that few Gothic authors besides Walpole, Radcliffe, Lewis, Mary Shelley, and Maturin abide in the memories of even the highly literate reading public is that the vast majority continued to practice faults which Mrs. Radcliffe generally remedied.

The major structural flaw in *Castles* is its "huddled" paragraphs. Within their amorphous bounds, Mrs. Radcliffe shifts abruptly from incident to incident to permeate a general lack of continuity with an inevitable distortion of emphasis. Such paragraphs do not pass muster as fast-moving description because they fail to bring the reader face to face with the variety of actions and reactions they barely take time to mention. No reader feels them happening. If the paragraph has some Gothic pretensions, it tries to live up to them with a crude pastiche of horrific details labeled and stuck together with the hope that they will somehow shock and surprise. A sneak attack, a fray, a defeat, the aftermath, and the reception of the bad news at home are recited as if they were part of chronicle history rather than of dramatic narrative.

The expedient justification for abrupt transition (within or without such paragraphs) baldly surfaces after the intrusively late appearance of Santmorin, whose generalized description is followed without a break by "new distress now broke upon the peace of Athlin. . . ." Things have in fact been much too peaceful for romantic adventure. We see through the disjointed anatomy of the paragraph to Mrs. Radcliffe's inner strainings after an exciting item to bolster her fading narrative.

The rhetorical and (for Ann Radcliffe) the nearly pictorial justification for structural discontinuity is the need for contrast. Mixed elements are violently yoked together and developed in disorderly sequence when the Count is told that he is rejected by Mary and—no dejection time allowed—his perspective and ours are shuttled off to a distant hill where we see a cloud which suddenly glistens into a flash of arms and the Baron's men.

The Castles of Athlin and Dunbayne

As Mrs. Radcliffe will learn—and she learns her lesson well—in order for contrast to be effective, it must be developed with some attention to the reciprocal effect each element has on the other. Other specialized rhetorical aids to fear and trembling introduced disparately in *Castles* flourish in concert in later novels. The piling up of prospective horrors combines with the memory of past evils (even remembered love tends to be a negative memory simply because it is always irrevocably lost) to remind the reader that any momentary rest from immediate oppression is only a prelude or condition for imagined evils infinitely more intolerable than anything which can actually happen to the heroine.

Malcolm's technique for tormenting Osbert provided Ann Radcliffe with the secret of her success: "He racked imagination for the invention of tortures equal to the force of his feelings; and he at length discovered that the sufferings of suspense are superior to those of the most terrible evils, when once ascertained, of which the contemplation affords to strong minds the means of endurance. He determined, therefore, that the Earl should remain confined in the tower, ignorant of his future destiny; and in the meantime should be allowed food only sufficient to keep him sensible of his wretchedness" (726).

Her ability to create and maintain an atmosphere of suspense through several pages of narrative otherwise largely lacking in dramatic interest established Mrs. Radcliffe's clear preeminence over her imitators. Her initial problem was to discover and manipulate rhetorical techniques that would intensify reader interest during these pages rather than allow it to dissipate into tedium. One of these techniques was to give the reader food for inference only sufficient to keep him sensible of the multiplicity of wretched circumstances and alternatives a heroine ignorant of her destiny was bound to contemplate. A more subtle and more dramatic method was to gradually enmesh the reader and the heroine together in an increasing awareness of these same circumstances and alternatives. But, in order for the reader to sympathize with the heroine, he had to get to know her—if only through the conventional situations of the sentimental novel. Then the rhetorical devices which aided the dramatic effect were accepted rather than seen through.

Even as early as *Castles* Mrs. Radcliffe had learned the secret of effective repetition. Three or four times in the body of a single paragraph she succinctly rephrases the particular combination of horrors that burns most fiercely in Matilda's résumé of alternatives after she has been given Malcolm's ultimatum: "Her mind shrunk from the idea of uniting the daughter to the murderer of the father." At times—as in the finely wrought if melodramatic tableau depicting Alleyn's colloquy with the ladies Matilda and Mary before he leaves to free Osbert—Mrs. Radcliffe indicates that she can manipulate a suggestive narrative account of the dramatic potential inherent in the sentimental convention of blushes and sidelong glances between lovers who must remain silent.

More often, however, when she strives to use sentimental convention to express a climactic confrontation between lovers, she falls back on exclamation marks to cover her dramatic ineptness: "As [Alleyn] pressed [Mary's picture] with impassioned tenderness to his lips, the tear of rapture trembled in his eye, and the romantic ardour of the moment was scarcely heightened by the actual presence of the beloved object, whose light step now stole upon his ear; and half turning, he beheld, not the picture, but the reality!—Surprised!—confused!—the picture fell from his hand" (750). The outer action is simply squandered away in Mrs. Radcliffe's hurry to illustrate inner anguish through rhetorical forms that replace rather than set off dramatic intensity. In 1789, she had not learned how to manipulate the patterns of suspense that were to distinguish her novels from her imitators'.

CHAPTER 4

The Sicilian Romance

IN *The Sicilian Romance* (1791), Mrs. Radcliffe's first representative Gothic novel, she largely discarded the mixed atmosphere and trappings of medieval and historical romance that she had adopted from Walpole and Leland. She chose instead to focus her talent for conjuring up natural and supernatural terrors on the sentimental heroine whose literary sufferings had been limited to domestic and premarital tribulations in the precedents set down by Richardson and his imitators. Although heroes now and then succumb to the sound of their own footsteps echoing through deserted corridors, the terrors induced by ghostly phenomena, banditti, a villainous father and as nearly a vicious suitor are suffered to better effect by the heroine. The father-villain figure, instead of being introduced as as a kind of *diabolus ex machina* whenever a dire event is required to try the heroine's (or hero's) sensibility, interacts with the other characters so that some dramatic tension is occasionally achieved. Ghostly effects occur more frequently and are more terrifying than in *Castles*, largely because Mrs. Radcliffe keeps us in suspense until the end concerning their major source. And it is the discovery of this pseudoghostly agency that unravels the mysteries of the natural as well as of the supernatural world and so ties them together. The action is further complicated by the addition of secondary villains, who continue to complement the archvillain, either as agents or fell opposites, in the novels which follow. There is also a not very successful attempt at introducing into the action a villainess, a lurid but nonetheless poorly integrated forerunner of the Marchesa di Vivaldi in *The Italian*. Her logical foil is the heroine's elderly female instructress and confidante, who, along with the Catholic church, its monasteries, convents, abbots and nuns, concludes the list of significant innovations in Mrs. Radcliffe's second novel.

I *Summary*

The setting of *The Sicilian Romance* is, as the title indicates, Sicily, toward the end of the sixteenth century. The exotic southern European background not only provided Mrs. Radcliffe with a better chance to indulge her descriptive talents but also kept these descriptions from incurring the censure of critics who had been sufficiently aware of the Scottish Highlands to recognize the inappropriateness of much of the decor used to set off the action in *Castles*. In this second novel, the Marquis of Mazzini and his present Marchioness are well matched in their evil dispositions; the former Marchioness, who had been a gentle and mild-tempered lady, had reputedly died under the oppressions of her cruel lord. Her daughters, Julia and Emilia, are living in the Mazzini castle with their guide and teacher, Madame Menon, a friend of the former Marchioness. While there is some initial attempt to distinguish the characters of the two daughters, Mrs. Radcliffe soon decided that one was sufficient for her purposes. Emilia barely appears during the course of the novel, except on occasion to weep in sympathy with Julia's distresses.

The second Marchioness, jealous of the beauty of her two step-daughters, keeps them in seclusion in the castle while she and her husband enjoy the artificial gaieties of the city. The daughters are quite content with their secluded lot and are, in fact, distressed when the Marquis and Marchioness descend on the castle to celebrate the coming of age of the Marquis's son and their brother, Ferdinand. The Marchioness, whose lewdness is well defined if not well detailed, is violently in love with young Hippolytus, who, however, is indifferent to her. He arrives in the entourage of the Marquis and Marchioness and is very soon in love with Julia, who tacitly returns his affection.

A little before the Marquis arrives, the ladies at the castle are frightened by a mysterious light they see in a deserted wing which had for many years been closed off from the rest of the building. A dying steward is about to impart some news of this light when he breathes his last. Ferdinand is told of the light on his arrival and investigates the south wing. After being exposed to a series of low moans, flickering lights, and crumbling masonry, he discovers nothing but his own terror. Ferdinand tells the Marquis of his ghostly adventure but at first receives only his father's rebuke for allowing himself to be moved by such childish fears. However, the Marquis then confesses that he himself had once been frightened in that same wing by the apparition of a man whom his father had killed there. Later (and just as inconsistently), the Marquis allays his servants' fears by leading a ghost hunt through the wing and by giving a few natural explanations for some of the apparently supernatural phenomena. His father's explanation puzzles Ferdinand, and it may be our hint that the Marquis has perhaps lied to his son about the ghostly visitation he had experienced.

Not long after Julia knows that Hippolytus loves her, she is told that she must prepare to marry Duke de Luovo, whose evil nature makes him a man after the Marquis's own heart and who is, consequently, an object of Julia's abhorrence. Ferdinand and Hippolytus talk Julia into running away with them in order to escape parental tyranny. After a trying midnight excursion through secret and musty underground chambers, they arrive outside the castle walls only to be met by the Marquis and his men. Ferdinand is imprisoned, Hippolytus escapes but is badly wounded, and Julia is shut up in her room. After Julia mysteriously escapes, Duke de Luovo sets off in pursuit but is soon captured by banditti, whose leader is none other than his own son; for the Duke's tyrannical authority had driven his son to crime. Finally released, the Duke spends a tedious time in pursuit of a young couple who turn out to be, not Julia and Hippolytus, but another couple who are also escaping from parental tyranny in order to marry.

Meanwhile, Madame Menon discovers the Marchioness keeping a tryst with a lover; and, while Madame disdains to betray the unfaithful Marchioness, she leaves under duress. After wandering about a bit, she discovers Julia hiding in a peasant's hut after she had been aided in her escape by her maidservant. Madame Menon and Julia then set out together, and they are pursued by a band of men who turn out to be, not the vassals of the Duke or Marquis, but the followers of the parent from whom the couple mistakenly caught by the Duke had been fleeing. The two women then seek sanctuary in a nunnery, where Julia discovers that "her favorite nun" (who relates her sad story of frustrated love) is Hippolytus's sister.

She soon dies, and Julia is then presented with new cause for woe when the Abbot refuses to turn her over to the Marquis (who by now is more or less besieging the nunnery) because his self-esteem has been outraged by the Marquis's peremptory insistence that he immediately surrender Julia. He would himself reserve her for a fate worse than the Marquis by making a nun of her. The Marquis hesitates to push his legal claim because the Abbot knows something about him which he has apparently obtained from the confessor of the dying steward, Vincent.

Like *Castles, The Sicilian Romance* ends with a bustle of running about and revelation. Ferdinand, who has escaped his father's dungeon, rescues Julia from the monastery; and, after a shipwreck, they are left safely for a while as we turn to the recovered Hippolytus, who has been following Julia's trail. After a time, he arrives at a ruin full of bandits, where he discovers and rescues Julia, only to be pursued by the Duke's men, whom Hippolytus holds off at a cave's entrance while Julia penetrates its depths. The cave eventually leads to a dungeon cell in which Julia discovers the supposedly dead Marchioness, her mother, who had been imprisoned there years ago when the Marquis had decided he wanted to marry the present Marchioness. The major mystery of the south wing is then explained: the lights and moans were in various ways associated with the Marchioness, whose dungeon is attached to the wing and whose keeper had been the dead steward, Vincent. Julia and the Marchioness are baffled in their attempt at escape. The Marquis then decides to poison the food of his former Marchioness in order to bury forever the evidence of the crime which the Abbot holds over his head. When the Marquis discovers his present Marchioness's infidelity and threatens her with a separation, she poisons him and kills herself, though not before he had brought the poisoned food to the imprisoned Marchioness. Ferdinand now reappears to search out both Julia and his mother, who had been rescued by Hippolytus before the poisoned food had been eaten and taken to a lighthouse where Ferdinand finds them in time for a joyous reunion which is soon followed by the marriage of Julia and Hippolytus.

This piling up of calamities and turns of fortune may suggest that there is a good deal of extrinsic action dramatically detailed so as to enliven the reader's sense of participation with the inner turmoil suffered by the oppressed heroes and heroines. But in much the same way that the sensitive lover is expected to recognize the shifting moods of his beloved without her speaking a word, so is the sensitive or conditioned reader expected to imagine the vividness of the outer action from the narrative outline of it which Mrs. Radcliffe provides. Or rather the reader's real concern is not supposed to be with the outer action at all but with the effects of this action on the sympathetic and usually passive recipients of it. The action and the surprises inherent in it are necessary to the psychological torments suffered by the heroine (most of all), but they are not in themselves important—nor does Mrs. Radcliffe's handling of them suggest that they are. The anticipation of a given event and the steps leading to it are significant because they develop the requisite condition of intolerable suspense which the action itself merely relieves rather than climaxes. As the author editorializes at appropriate junctures, uncertainty about what *may* happen is far more distressing than anything that does happen.

II *The Villains*

The redundancy of villains oppressing the sentimental heroine is the major significant innovation in *The Sicilian Romance*. The archvillain Mazzini is cast after the fashion of Malcolm, but he has the added attraction of participating directly in the affairs of the heroine through his role as parental authority. The theme of parental authority as a paramount and often tyrannical force in the life of the sentimental heroine is developed in a variety of subordinate incidents that are either incorporated into the narrative progression or interpolated as flashbacks into the lives of Madame Menon, Hippolytus's sister, and the former Marchioness. The tenor of these incidents simply accords with the motif developed by the main story line: fathers or guardians are generally misguided or self-interested in deciding the marital destinies of their daughters or wards. They may not all be compendiums of evil, as Mazzini is, but they are usually blinkered by social or economic prejudices into discountenancing or misconceiving the significance of love in marriage. Parallel to Mazzini is the Marquis whose chase after his eloping daughter introduces the confusion which verges on the dramatic until it finally exits into the ludicrous. We are left with the impression that the Sicilian countryside is strewn with runaway lovers hotly pursued by outraged fathers or fiancés.

While Mazzini's character suffers through much of the same

kind of generalization that had stereotyped Malcolm as the traditional vice figure, he gains enough psychological reality to stand as the first truly representative Radcliffean villain. The usual formulas apply—he is imperious, arrogant, impetuous, impatient, voluptuous, ambitious, proud, revengeful, suspicious—and, of course, self-interested. A few other characteristics are added to Mazzini's repertory: he is unresponsive to music; he is often abstracted from his present surroundings; he is an empirical skeptic who ridicules the credulous who believe in the possibility of the supernatural; he is not at home in convivial gatherings, even of his own making.

What brings Mazzini to some semblance of life is the opposition he suffers not from his apparent foes, the representatives of the good, but from his own evil passions and from the like passions in his logical counterparts in evil, the Abbot and, most excruciatingly, his Marchioness, whom he loves with a "romantic fondness." While the good actors are passive (except when fleeing), evil natures are not only actively self-destructive but also unwittingly work against their own interests by bringing about the triumph of good. The salvation of Osbert in *Castles* had depended on the victory (in Malcolm) of one vicious passion over another, and Julia's salvation depends on a like victory of vanity over avarice in the self-interested calculations of the Abbot: she "received from his pride that protection which neither his principle nor his humanity would have granted." While Mrs. Radcliffe's esthetic purpose is to emphasize the pathos of Julia's intolerable situation, her ethical message fits conveniently into the display of contrarious passions at work within the breast of the Abbot, as well as in the exchanges between him and the Marquis. The Abbot, for all his hysterical and rather effeminate vanity, fails to frustrate the Marquis nearly so much as does the latter's irrational passion for the adulterous Marchioness, who is herself subject to fits of passion which prevent her from furthering her designs on Hippolytus.

Love, as Mrs. Radcliffe everywhere illustrates in her heroes and heroines, must be founded in disinterestedness, like sensibility, and mutual esteem. Consequently, the only variation on love a twisted and self-interested nature like the Marquis's can experience is its perversion as jealous and lustful passion. When he discovers the Marchioness's infidelity, he reacts according to such passion rather than to any principle:

This information lighted up the wildest passions of his nature; his former sufferings faded away before the stronger influence of the present misfortune, and it seemed as if he had never tasted misery till now. To suspect the wife he doted on with romantic fondness, on whom he centred all his firmest hopes of happiness, and for whose sake he had committed the crime which embittered even his present moments, and which would involve him in still deeper guilt —to find *her* ungrateful to his love, and a traitress to his honour— produced a misery more poignant than any his imagination had conceived. He was torn by contending passion, and opposite resolutions: —now he resolved to expiate her guilt with her blood—and now he melted in all the softness of love. Vengeance and honour bade him strike to the heart which had betrayed him, and urged him instantly to the deed—when the idea of her beauty—her winning smiles—her fond endearments, stole upon his fancy, and subdued his heart. . . . (69–70)

While Mrs. Radcliffe's overriding concern with her heroine's sensibility allows her space only to hint at the fact, we should assume that the villain suffers more through his viciousness than does anyone else. A heroine has her good works, firm principles, and conscious worth to solace her in hours of misery. The villain has nothing but his viciousness to reflect on, perhaps to question, and finally to condemn himself for before he passes on to his just deserts.

When the Marquis does question the merits of evildoing a little before his death, he is by no means on the way to a good act of contrition. Mrs. Radcliffe wants him to suffer the pangs of recognizing that his life has been misled from beginning to end before he dies. And, lest we think that the Marquis is at all redeemed by the compassion which leads him to spare his present Marchioness ("Pity now suspended his vengeance"), we are told that the motive force behind this deviation from vengeance is an "absurd fondness" which caused his passion to increase when he realized he had lost his wife's love. "The very circumstances which should have aroused his aversion, by a strange perversity of disposition, appeared to heighten his passion. . . ."

The Marquis possesses a conscience, which humanizes him just enough for him to suffer ghostly hallucinations without leading him to repent fully his premeditated poisoning of his first Marchioness until he is at his very last gasp. The villain always breaks down at the end; but, since his life has been an implicit compact with the devil, we need not suppose that the moment of truth or self-awareness is meant to save his soul. By pointing out the moral of his evil life, he merely fulfills his allegorical obligation to the reader: "Heaven had made that woman the instrument of its justice, whom I make the instrument of my crimes." The rhetorical balance and poetic justice of the sentiment make up for the fact that it is not altogether true.

III *The Heroine*

The heroine has still not come into her own as the nearly exclusive medium through which the reader achieves his perspective on the Radcliffean world; but a discernible attempt is made at eliciting, if not developing, Julia's character. Mrs. Radcliffe is consistent with eighteenth-century precedent when she exposes her characters to situations in which they are allowed to become themselves according to predictions implicit in their initial description as types rather than as individuals. Julia lives up to our expectations; but, if we attune ourselves to the conventional sensibility Mrs. Radcliffe was writing for, we see that fate must aid character on occasion in order for these expectations to be fulfilled. The precarious tightrope which the heroine walks in her progress through a Radcliffean novel requires her to balance herself between the villain and the hero so that she does not fall into the clutches of the one or surrender to protestations of love from the other. The Gothic terrors evolved either directly or indirectly by the villain have their predictable and obvious effect on the heroine's sensibility. In her attempts to avoid them, she is sporadically faced with a temptation to accept the hero's protection by marrying him before conditions are absolutely ideal. Julia comes closer than any of her sister heroines (with the possible exception of Ellena in *The Italian*) to falling into the arms of her hero before the time is ripe and decorous.

From Richardson's *Clarissa* through Fielding's *Tom Jones* to Austen's *Pride and Prejudice*, an eloping heroine was likely running toward a disaster that was at least as certain as the tribulations in store for her if she decided not to run. And yet she often ran, even though the domestic tyranny she thereby escaped was not nearly so oppressive as the terrors which the Radcliffean heroine was tempted to shun by a precipitous marriage. Julia is twice presented with the temptation to run off and marry Hippolytus. The first time she gives in; and, while an eighteenth-century audience might sympathize with her for doing so, they had few significant precedents for predicting a happy conclusion to the marriage she came dangerously close to consummating.

Mrs. Radcliffe frustrates her escape not only to plunge her into despair and additional tribulations but also to save her from the consequences of a decision which, in spite of circumstances, was not ideally justified. When she does escape, she is not required to pay the price of an inauspicious marriage in order to carry it off. And, when she is next faced with the same decision, she demurs. A hasty marriage is as dangerous in the long run to a girl's peace of mind as the terrors and oppressions which seem to justify it are in the short run. The reader whose moral sensibility is as discriminating as his esthetic responses would find Julia's narrow escape from a marriage of expedience as harrowing as her experience in the chamber of decaying corpses, where her sense of delicacy is tried in quite another way.

Julia's vacillation from steadfast principle is largely the result of her brother's assent to what her heart desires. But it also suggests the sanguine temperament which Mrs. Radcliffe criticizes her for when she too quickly falls in love with Hippolytus. She suffers, like all Radcliffean heroines, from "an extreme sensibility" which will have to be moderated by experience in order for her to develop the firmness she finally shows when she looks at the tyrannical Abbot "with steadfast eye" and succinctly points out to him the weakness of principle which tempts him to knuckle under to the Marquis. Even more suggestive of newly acquired or perceived spiritual resource is the "strange and sudden exertion of fortitude" with which she denies the Duke's suit in spite of her father's wishes. It is, then, not quite fair to say that Mrs. Radcliffe fails to suggest some expansion of native moral fiber in her heroines. The trials and errors that her sensibility exposes her to cause the young lady to grow a bit. The growth is hardly noticeable because it is described in conventional scenes and confrontations which are themselves couched in narrative clichés rather than dramatically developed. The author's inventive powers—and they are often surprisingly strong and discriminatingly applied when she deals with the dire alternatives faced by the heroine—did not work through the medium of realistic detail or extrinsic action. Mrs. Radcliffe requires from her readers the same kind of susceptibility to a vague but standard intimation that her heroines required from their heroes.

IV Gothic Effects

Macabre and terrifying incidents are much more abundant in *The Sicilian Romance* than they had been in *Castles*, where there is hardly an occurrence that smacks of the supernatural. Most importantly, there is the reservoir of mysterious phenomena contained in the deserted south wing that is finally explained by the discovery of the former Marchioness. Mrs. Radcliffe supplements this main chamber of horrors with the unnatural villainies perpetrated or planned by the Marquis, the Duke, and the various groups of banditti, replete with Salvatorean caves, that abound in the Sicilian landscape. The hairbreadth or frustrated escapes take place against a gloomy background, either of forest pathways or of castle corridors. The obscure unreality of the decor is heightened by the nightmarish tension between the need for headlong flight and the obstacles, like locked doors and unworkable keys, which inevitably impede the fugitives on their way. There seems to be a kind of diabolical agency at work in the decaying stones and rotten wood of the Gothic structure that emphasizes an easily conceivable relationship between the villain who owns the castle and the devil to whom, in all probability, he has pledged himself.

The predictable effect of several such flights, the recapturings and consequent escapes, on the tender sensibilities of the heroine is that even a circumstance some distance removed from actual horror can "conjure up a terror which reason could not subdue." If a heroine who nearly faints at the sight of a bloody splotch on the wall is set down in a room full of decaying corpses, her "reactions can easily be conceived"—to use the words with which Mrs. Radcliffe often pleads her way out of a descriptive chore.

Mrs. Radcliffe seemingly exhausts the possibility for an intensely traumatic response to an actual corpse or villainous act by previously arousing her heroine's excitable nature to its utter limits in a state of sheer anticipation. Since so many more events can be contemplated than can actually occur, the method is probably justified by its effect on the reader: he goes through more than mere action when he lives in the heroine's imagination.

Now and then we may want some terrific detail in the manner of Lewis or Maturin. But, if we consider the relative ineffectiveness of Mrs. Radcliffe's description of the macabre when Julia and Ferdinand enter the bandit's charnel room, "a receptacle for the murdered bodies of the unfortunate people who had fallen into the hands of the banditti," we see not only that she fails to enliven the ghostly tableau by fulfilling its gory potential but that she enervates it by her verbiage and euphemism. The psychology of *anticipated* rather than *executed* horrors is necessarily her forte. If we have done our part as conventionally attuned eighteenth-century readers would—aware of the power of suggestion, association, imagination, and memory—we can sublimely if obscurely share the heroine's reaction to a generalized scene of horror without being told very much about it. If we demand more substance with our shadows, we can find it in the straightforward delineations of the German horror school, which dealt in concrete forms of blood and bones for the sake of readers who could not accommodate their esthetics of terror to the delicate psychology of a sentimental heroine.

Both Gothic castle and abbey achieve their classic forms in later novels, though they first appear in concert here, along with the secular and spiritual villains who generally oversee them. There are also some rudimentary attempts at suggesting both the horror and the beauty of the Catholic church, though quite uncharacteristically the best though brief account of an awed reaction to the sublime inherent in a ruined abbey is allowed to the Duke during his inflated and meaningless search after the escaped Julia. There are two or three set pieces which editorialize into the dramatic action the conditions under which the reader may (and even should) accept the accoutrements of the supernatural for the real thing. The psychological state of mind in which Julia finds herself on being removed to the south wing by the malicious and self-interested Marchioness goes a long way toward forgiving her for the unnamed but inferable "images of terror" that fill her mind whenever low groans and flickering lights impinge on her ears and eyes and work their supernatural effects on her overwrought sensibility.

Mrs. Radcliffe consistently explains the superstitious misconceptions of an otherwise rational individual whom emotional duress had driven to confuse the worlds of sense and hallucination—a confusion which the empirical psychology of the day aided rather than dissipated. Imprisoned by his father, Ferdinand hears a series of moans which he believes issues from the departed shade of his grandfather's victim. In a reaction better applied to a heroine, Ferdinand supposes he would die of very horror if the spirit itself should appear in his cell:

The mind of Fedinand was highly superior to the general influence of superstition; but, in the present instance, such strong correlative circumstances appeared, as compelled even incredulity to yield. He had himself heard strange and awful sounds . . . he received from his father a dreadful secret relative to them. . . . All these recollections presented to Ferdinand a chain of evidence too powerful to be resisted; and he could not doubt that the spirit of the dead had for once been permitted to revisit the earth, and to call down vengeance on the descendants of the murderer. (38)

When the more sophisticated among Radcliffean characters give in to such fears, they are usually well justified both by the empirical evidence available and by their own physical and psychological condition. More importantly, the reader himself, who recognizes the supernatural possibility (given the evidence available), experiences emotions kindred to those suffered by the hero.

Earlier in the novel Madame Menon is asked by Julia whether supernatural intercession in earthly affairs is possible. The sage Madame tends to justify Ferdinand in advance when she says that a just and beneficent Providence may on occasion see fit to adjust temporal affairs should they become unmanageable by the natural agencies designed to carry out God's will. The moral appended to Radcliffean novels generally allows this same supernatural overseer His place in quelling evil and rewarding good, though, as it happens, He had not been required to disrupt the normal sequence of things since, in a fundamentally good world, evil crumbles and merit succeeds. Madame Menon, consistent with both religious and empirical psychology, points out that many things which are indisputably true cannot be understood by the limited minds of man. She would never deny the possibility of *benevolent* supernatural causation or of the "disembodied spirits" it may use as agency.

The perfect foil for the Madame Menon–Julia dialogue on the spirit world is the similar Mazzim–Ferdinand exchange during which the Marquis, whose empiricism is quite sense-bound, denies the supernatural and thereby proves his pride, his insensibility, and, so it seems, his irreligion. The collective inference is that evil acts perpetrated against good men are not the result of supernatural agency because such agency is inevitably good. Evil will eventually be found to stem from unnatural but still earthly agents. Other supernatural effects—indifferently terrible rather than actively malignant—are finally tracked down to their source in the natural and, usually, the trivial. Aiding and abetting this source is the overactive or overwrought imagination of the individual who initially misconceives what he sees or hears as somehow associated with an infernally supernatural power.

The point to be made—and it is worth reiterating because it is traditionally missed in evaluating Mrs. Radcliffe's supernatural effects—is that, from the beginning, she gave her readers and critics fair warning that the more dramatic supernatural effects woven into the fabric of her sentimental novels will finally be rationalized according to her moral sense. They would not be groomed to fit relatively superficial esthetic demands made by romantically inclined readers who can believe, for instance, that in some literal (and un-Blakean) sense Milton was of the Devil's party without knowing it.

V *Technique*

The technical crudities of *Castles* are to some extent refined by Mrs. Radcliffe's increasing recognition that the rhetoric of terror inspired fear and trembling in the reader only when manipulated by or for characters who were at least conventionally human. Julia is an attempt at portraying a sentimental heroine; the allied attempt at developing a secondary or foil heroine in Emilia was as yet beyond Mrs. Radcliffe's powers of execution. With the introduction of a strong secondary villain in opposition to the Marquis, the heroine's fate depends, as it will most thrillingly in later novels, on the opposition between evil and evil rather than between evil and good. The role of the hero is really shared by Ferdinand and Hippolytus, though the consequent dilution of the character in no way conflicts with its usual presentation. The Duke, however, is a feeble counterpart of the allegorical Malcolm, while his sentimental reflections render him inconsistently sympathetic besides. The attempt at developing a sophisticated guide and confidante in Madame Menon is likewise marred when, for all her customary aplomb, she runs fleeing with the rest at a moan or a bit of crumbled masonry.

The Radcliffean prose style shows signs of developing as a medium for the luxuriant scenic and Gothic descriptions which fill the later novels. Sublime scenery is used not only to backdrop a fleeing heroine but also to solace her with thoughts of God in the midst of her trials. The compendium of evils, the choice from among dire alternatives, the thought of grief to qualify every resurgent joy continue to stand for psychological probes and cosmic irony. Hippolytus's dilemma at one juncture typifies Mrs. Radcliffe's dramatic ideal: "A choice of errors only lay before him."

The most memorable and dramatic scene in the novel is the confrontation between the Abbot and the Marquis during the siege of the convent. The debate between these two evil agents is a precursor of later and greater dialogues between more or less villainous characters (like La Motte and Montalt in *The Romance of the Forest* and Schedoni and the Marchesa in *The Italian*). Because it is dramatic, not only in itself but also in its bearing on the heroine, it escapes the limitations—sometimes verging on the ludicrous—built into the still lifes or tableaux which depict comparable climactic scenes where the suggested pathos or terror of the occasion is supposed to overcome the reader's demands for credibility. Hippolytus lets us relish to the full the set piece in which Julia languishes in the bandits' clutches before he rushes in to become her savior. Later we listen and watch with a hidden Julia while the Marquis torments her mother in an adjoining cell.

What Mrs. Radcliffe had discovered is that it makes a difference through whom vicarious suffering is experienced by the reader. The lover viewing his loved one at the mercy of licentious men or the daughter viewing her mother mistreated by her father compounds the terror potential of the same scene merely described or viewed by a relatively indifferent observer. The reader suffers both what is felt by the observer and by the dearly beloved that he observes. For the sake of such supercharged emotional tableaux Mrs. Radcliffe was willing to risk dramatic improbability. She may of course fail egregiously. The sentimental set piece in which Hippolytus's sister, Julia's "favorite nun," is allowed to die in the presence of her former lover is too pat to be pathetic. It is neither integrated with the narrative nor with the conventional sympathies we might muster for Julia, who is the agency through whom the scene is narrated and felt.

The persistent use of these tableaux for dramatic effect emphasizes Mrs. Radcliffe's concern with psychological, rather than chronological, time. Her characters come to a standstill, much like the figures in a Lorrain or Rosa painting, to observe rather than participate in the action or scenic decor around them. After an exhausting flight from terror to a given villa, the heroine takes time to enjoy the contrasted beauty of her present surroundings before succumbing to fatigue. While physically inconceivable, such a display of sensibility is dramatically appropriate and psychologically credible in a world where mental and emotional actions and reactions take precedence over the likelihood of merely extrinsic physical cause-effect relationships. When Hippolytus contemplates his loved one in the clutches of the banditti, "joy and terror" are allowed to animate his bosom in heightened emotional contrast before he degenerates to the subordinate activity of simply rescuing Julia.

Toward the conclusion of the novel, the outer action becomes more turbulent in correspondence with the breathtaking back and forth of grief and joy experienced by the heroine and reader. Together, they signify the intolerable tension just this side of chaos in the inner as in the outer world. The climactic point of the novel is reached when an event, which once would have aroused Julia from grief to at least a pleasing melancholy, has no positive effect on her. The descent to this abysm of despair has been gradually made along an inverted spiral of psychic disasters ever more rapidly whirlpooling her into an emotional vortex where joy itself occasions only indifference because of the many precedents suggesting that it is only a prelude to misery. The real risk which the sentimental Gothic heroine typically incurred was not physical but psychical: her delicate sensibility was consistently in danger of becoming either callous or chaotic in response to the external range of passions it lived through.

CHAPTER 5

The Romance of the Forest

*T*HE *Romance of the Forest* (1792) is Ann Radcliffe's first major novel, as well as the one which established her reputation as the first among her era's writers of romance. There is surprisingly little essential difference in characterization, Gothic decor, or plot outline to distinguish this novel from its predecessors. Its superior merit lies in the expansive and subtle use which the author makes of these elements so that the characters are relatively well realized, the Gothic decor is blended into the sensibility of the reader rather than imposed upon it, and the plot is an intricate and often dramatic series of congruent incidents and living tableaux, not a congeries of barely related and stillborn scenes and surprises.

Adeline, the heroine, is almost always the central attraction, for even the villain Montalt, and his co-villains, fade off into the wings on occasion so that she can expand the spectrum of her sensibility by reacting to an increased range of pitiable or sympathetic situations, as well as to the terrible ones which contrast and condition them. The mixed characters of Adeline's sometime protectors, Pierre and Madame La Motte; the dramatic exchanges between La Motte and Montalt; and the use of the La Mottes' son, Louis, as a subtle foil to Adeline's preferred lover, Theodore, are all substantial signs of Mrs. Radcliffe's increasing dexterity at developing and filling in her plot through a subtle and not always predictable interaction of personalities and passions.

Her supreme achievement in this novel is probably the use she makes of stock Gothic features like the ominously prophetic dream and the fragmented manuscript full of intimated horrors. Conditioned by the midnight hour and by the solitary room in which Adeline dreams and reads, they serve as a continuing parallel or counterpoint to the real horrors which oppress or threaten the heroine. More credibly and effectively than in *The Sicilian Ro-*

mance, these parallel worlds of supernatural and natural terrors converge in the *expliqué*-as-revelation which concludes the novel and proves, as usual, that evil in this world is traceable to the acts of evil men who are inevitably exposed by the goodness of divine Providence.

I *Summary*

A brief outline of this relatively accessible novel should be a sufficient background for the analysis which follows. Pierre and Madame La Motte leave Paris to escape the legal consequences of La Motte's shady financial transactions. Almost immediately La Motte is set upon by a group of armed men who grant him life and freedom only on condition that he take with him Adeline, the heroine, who consequently accompanies the La Mottes to a ruined abbey, in the midst of a forest, where they soon set up housekeeping, though not before a few fluttering owls had predicted the ghostly potential of their new home. Local accounts, as reported by the garrulous servant, Peter, confirm this potential with mysterious stories of a murder perhaps perpetrated by the abbey's owner. Adeline, we are now told, had spent her life in a convent until her supposed father's impatience at her refusal to become a nun caused him to remove her just prior to her being given to La Motte.

La Motte's son Louis soon appears, falls in love with Adeline, and is followed by the Marquis de Montalt, who owns the abbey, clearly has some power over La Motte, and also wants Adeline. Theodore, the true hero, appears in Montalt's retinue. La Motte occasionally makes mysterious visits to a local tomb which causes his wife to suspect that he is carrying on an intrigue with Adeline, who thereby loses Madame's friendship.

Theodore unaccountably leaves, Montalt becomes more insistent, and Adeline dreams of midnight wanderings in darkened corridors, a pursuing figure, a dying man in his coffin. The dream is realized a little later when she discovers a secret door in her room that leads her to the same chamber wherein the dying man had lain, and where she soon discovers the manuscript—apparently written by this same man—that will intermittently evoke her pity and terror. Convinced that La Motte will aid Montalt in his dishonorable designs on her, Adeline resolves to escape with Peter; but, instead, she is whisked off to Montalt's château where his

Comus-like attempts at seduction fail long enough for her to escape with Theodore, who has absented himself without leave from his regiment (which is led by Montalt). The Marquis eventually recovers Adeline, sends her back to the La Mottes, and has a wounded Theodore put into prison. After some vacillation, La Motte refuses to murder Adeline, as the Marquis now desires; instead, he aids her to escape to another part of the country. She is there nursed back to health by a family named La Luc, which is soon discovered to be Theodore's family.

Again, the action of the novel is brought to a bustling conclusion with much anxiety and revelation. La Motte, also in jail through Montalt's malice, and Theodore are freed when Montalt is found guilty of having killed his half-brother, Adeline's real father, who had been the writer of the manuscript and, apparently, the prototype of the dying man in her dream. Montalt had not known her parentage until he had discovered a family seal on a letter she had sent to Theodore. He had then decided to kill her in order to retain the wealth he had previously killed her father to gain. Montalt, who dies horribly but contritely, wills his lands and money to Adeline, who marries Theodore and settles down for a lifetime of bliss enhanced by the contrasted terrors she had lived through.

II   *The Heroine*

Adeline plummets into La Motte's protective custody with much of the force of the giant helmet into the courtyard of Otranto. She is born into the fable full grown but unidentified. La Motte's reiterated remarks on the romantic unreality of it all suggest either Ann Radcliffe's embarrassed awareness of the strain she was putting on her reader's sense of probability, or, more likely, her invitation to her reader to enter a world where improbabilities are the stuff reality is made of. Adeline discovers her identity before our eyes. It is an identity which is more fully revealed by her dreams than it is by the facts of her life as she knows them. Her consistent lament is that she has no relative to whom she can turn with the hope of gaining the aid and sympathy which her supposed father had denied her. When she discovers that a minor character (though a good man), Verneuil, is distantly related to her, her reaction is at once incredulous and ecstatic. She moves through two false fathers—both Adeline and the reader are allowed to rest for a while under the terrible illusion that none other than Montalt had begotten her with a nun he had seduced —before she finally arrives at the truth which her sympathetic identification with the miserable writer of the manuscript had predicted.

Before she finally establishes that first basis for self-definition, she justifiably laments not only her friendless (and relativeless) state but also the equivocal actions and sentiments she notes in those who seemingly befriend her. The La Mottes inspire her guileless love; they then suspect her motives and betray her trust. Before them, the church had insidiously attempted to gain her soul against her conscience, while her supposed father had consistently betrayed her faith in their natural bond by his unnatural acts toward her. Peter promises to aid her in an escape attempt which results in her being placed absolutely in Montalt's power. Even Theodore (like Hippolytus before him) seems to betray the confidence and incipient love he had inspired in her by disappearing.

With all these temptations to misanthropy, Adeline preserves her resilient sensibility and her ultimate confidence in the innate benevolence of mankind and in the Providence directing its affairs. No heroine—not even Emily in *Udolpho* (who does have Annette at any rate, and has had St. Aubert)—is quite so alone and unprepared amid the persecutions Mrs. Radcliffe inflicts on her as is Adeline, nor is any other heroine thereby so tempted to betray her sensibility by hardening it. The major sign that she has preserved this sensibility is her reaction to the manuscript that, with retrospective dramatic irony, turns out to be her father's.

As Adeline asserts at the start (and repeats at the end of the novel), she was designed by a good Providence to unravel the mystery of the manuscript and of the abbey which would provide her with a real father, while baffling the villain who had destroyed this father and sought to destroy her and those who had become dear to her. The point is that a virtuous sensibility *is* a supernatural agency which can be afflicted by man-made evils but never conquered or hardened by them. And that is the moral of the piece which, to the critics' esthetic apprehension, rendered its horrors and extravagances unobjectionable.

A detailed account of the compounded horrors that impinge on Adeline's sensibility at about the time she finds the manuscript illustrates Mrs. Radcliffe's virtuosity at counterpointing the worlds of real and unreal fears. The image of past horrors evoked by the manuscript predict the future horrors which Adeline and her readers can suppose Montalt has in store for her. Her kindred sensibility responds to the pitiable condition of the long-dead man, her father; and, while her disinterestedness may (at first) prevent her from reading her fate in his, the reader is under no such moral restraint. The inarticulate exclamations of suffering reiterated through the oft-interrupted reading of the manuscript are anticipated echoes of those we may shortly expect from Adeline, once Montalt has his way with her. Mrs. Radcliffe has conditioned the reader for this converging parallel between unnatural and supernatural fears by gradually reducing Adeline to the psychological state of aloneness which, for a while, the La Mottes had seemed to relieve. La Motte's sullenness, his wife's spitefulness, Adeline's intuitive fears of Montalt, the recurrent fear that her supposed father may be lurking somewhere in the forest (as he is always in the background of her imagination)—all these signs and intimations of rejection or of obscure malice contribute to the overwrought state which aids in producing the apparitions of her dreams and fancy when she retires to indulge her aloneness in the small room that symbolizes it.

III *Specimen Gothic Decor*

The room deserves special comment, since in variant forms (as tower or dungeon) it appears in all major Radcliffean novels; it serves ambiguously as a retreat from the real world and as a vestibule leading directly, through dream or fancy or secret panel, to the unreal. In this world of memory, imagination, and association, the heroine expresses her sensibility through a much wider range of impassioned reaction to grief, melancholy, or fear than can be decorously or conveniently displayed in the real world. The happiest function of the room is to serve as a retreat from oppression into melancholy, which can there be indulged "at leisure." Partly in support of that function, the dormer window often looks out onto nature, sublime or beautiful (or both by turns), which is a usual antidote to most humanly induced horrors. Nature's efficacy stops short of settling a heroine's superstitious fears of what may lie beyond a hidden panel or unlockable second door, behind a black veil, under a black pall, in an old chest, or in an obscure closet off in the corner. In the room's less happy function as a Radcliffean looking glass rather than escape hatch, the heroine only walks away from the routine unpleasantness of the sentimental cast—parental tyranny and villain-lovers—into the ethos of the ghostly sublime, where the horrors are intensified by the obscurity of their source, which keeps them from empirical rationalization.

Consequently, the ultimate effect of the room, in its silence, solitude, and obscurity, is to refocus the heroine's attention and anticipations on another set of distressful objects. She has escaped for the moment the actual world, redundant with villainies, to an ideal world which nonetheless has a kind of semireality behind its illusoriness. That is, it contains actual objects that cause the illusions which trouble the heroine's distempered imagination. And they are often dreadful enough—as is, for instance, the rusted dagger that Adeline finds, whose truly horrible associations are not fully realized until at the end of the novel we discover that this dagger had very likely been used to kill her father. We know—though Adeline does not—that the skeleton itself (which had been discovered by La Motte, who said nothing of it) is somewhere in those underground vaults waiting for her to stumble over it anytime after she stumbles over the dagger. Mrs. Radcliffe's own delicate sensibilities might have suggested to her that the mere anticipation of such an event was enough to conjure up the appropriate dread in her reader's mind, while actually having her heroine stumble over the skeleton of her father might have seemed indecorous, even verging on the obscenely decadent.

The heroine's customary aloneness, timidity, and smallness are emphasized by the enveloping darkness and decay of Adeline's room, which suggest vastness in space and antiquity in time—Burkean conditions for that sublime which has a terror in it. Even the flickering light accentuates rather than dissipates the gloom by pointing up the tenuous connection she has with the daylight world. Whatever might seem positive and protective about the room is rendered flimsy and minuscule: "The wind was high, and as it whistled through the desolate apartment, and shook the feeble doors, she often started. . . ." Doors are never feeble when they stand between a heroine and escape, though they may be old and massive, with their iron locks rusted into place.

Her spirits plus the vast room full of decaying furniture oppress her with melancholy, yet she is unwilling to sleep because she fears a recurrence of her former nightmares. She reads but is unable to forget her problems; she leans pensively on her arm, abstracted, and "sometimes [she] even thought she heard sighs through the pauses of the gust." Mrs. Radcliffe's flowing and reciprocating periods assist the gradual but vacillating rise toward our accepting supernatural possibility—a kind of rocking effect echoing the movement from static contemplation through active imagining to rational explication. The process is repeated until explication is impossible and until the imagination exits instead into mystery and its consequent terrors. But not immediately: "she checked these illusions, which the hour of night and her own melancholy imagination conspired to raise."

The author deftly portrays a certain willingness, induced by melancholy and sheer lassitude, to surrender to supernatural suggestion and to the rational rejoinder which obliges the heroine to accept a natural explanation until she can no longer perceive a basis for it. By assigning natural causes to initial and relatively superficial ghostly effects, Mrs. Radcliffe builds the reader's confidence in the heroine's customary good sense and in the acuteness of her empirical perceptions and rational inferences. She is not taken in very easily; and, when she is taken in, the reader feels that the possible causes in nature have been exhausted. Lesser compositors of supernatural feints and tricks, the writers of mere horror tales, did not have the tact or discrimination to build toward an effect by seemingly withdrawing from it.

Adeline's unwillingness to pursue a plausible logic to its unnatural conclusion is correspondingly illustrated in the actual world when she implicitly chides herself for suspecting Montalt of murder on the flimsy evidence of intuition and mere gossip. And later her good sense deepens her blushing confusion when La Motte points out to her that the conclusions she had arrived at through eavesdropping were unwarranted by what she had actually heard. On one hand, Mrs. Radcliffe wants us aware of the circumspect rationality of the heroine so that, when she does finally deviate into irrational superstition, we are willing to accompany her. On the other hand, she wants us aware of the resurgent sensibility and overactive imagination of the heroine which, after all, mislead her as often as they leap to correct inference.

IV *Suspense*

By using reason and common sense as persistent foils or counterpoints to excessive sensibility or imagniation, Mrs. Radcliffe not only solicits the reader's confidence in Adeline's point of view but also "wiredraws" the suspense—which is her prime esthetic object and achievement: "As she sat musing, her eyes fixed on the opposite wall, she perceived the arras, with which the room was hung, wave backward and forward; she continued to observe it for some minutes, and then rose to examine it farther. It was moved by the wind; and she blushed at the momentary fear it had excited; but she observed that the tapestry was more strongly agitated in one particular spot than elsewhere, and a noise that seemed something more than the wind issued thence." (121)

We are gradually being led into the supernatural by real but at least unusual (if not unnatural) occurrences. Nonetheless, Mrs. Radcliffe is giving a hint to the perspicacious reader that he should not let his fancy or his irrational (or esthetic) hopes and fears lead him too far astray. After further probing of the arras, Adeline discovers the hidden but natural cause of the unnatural phenomenon, though even the natural cause has an eerie suggestiveness about it as she perceived "the wall behind shake under her hand" and as "she lifted the arras, and discovered a small door, whose loosened hinges admitted the wind, and occasioned the noise she had heard." This is a natural explanation after all, but it borders on the discovery of other effects that may not be so easily explained. When Adeline opens the door and enters another chamber, she moves through Alice's looking glass into a world where, so it seems, anything can happen—and, with positive trepidation, the reader hopes that it does.

Mrs. Radcliffe again illustrates the subtlety of her suspense technique by introducing an association which suggests the possibility she does not immediately fulfill: on entering the chamber, Adeline "instantly remembered her dreams." Instead of jumping to an easy identity between the dream and the real chamber, the author holds the dream in solution, and the reader in suspense, as Adeline indicates her rational discrimination under duress by allowing that it was not after all like *that* chamber, "yet it gave her a confused remembrance of one through which she had passed." We are not yet there, but we likely will be very soon. Meanwhile, we can anticipate the event, while avidly wondering at the same time precisely when Adeline will stumble over the skeleton we know is lurking somewhere about these dark dank corridors and vaults. She sees another door, gathers courage, and moralizes to herself: "A mystery seems to hang over these chambers . . . which it is perhaps my lot to develop; I will, at least, see to what that door leads." As it turns out, the moral fatalism which justifies her curiosity does not actually unfold the mystery by leading to the Marquis's conviction for his brother's murder in a court of law; for empirical evidence from another source is required for that. But he is discovered and condemned long before the anticlimactic appearance of his accusers by the imagination of the reader which Adeline's further explorations will inspire toward a correct prediction of the Marquis's guilt. The accusers are themselves a kind of *expliqué*; but, like all *expliqué*, they are largely irrelevant. Adeline unfolds the mystery where it counts—in the mind of the reader.

Prophetic dreams require no *expliqué* because they have both empirical and literary confirmation in psychology and in Homer. They are either true to life or to convention; in any case, Mrs. Radcliffe (and her followers) accepted them without explanation, though with no real insistence that there was a supernatural influence behind them. Eventually, Adeline arrives at the very chamber of her dream; she is overcome with superstitious dread; she stumbles over something just as the moon disappears—a spotted, rusty dagger. She looks for something else that "might confirm or destroy the dreadful suspicions which now rushed upon her mind." But she sees only the accoutrements of the Gothic sublime—a "great chair with broken arms," a shattered table, "a confused heap of things" which seem in their dissolution and obscurity a pile of old lumber but which gradually resolve their chaos into a ghostly semblance of "a broken bedstead, with some decayed remnants of furniture covered with dust and cobwebs, and which seemed, indeed, as if they had not been moved for many years."

Either through artistic ineptness or a unique sense of the dramatic moment Mrs. Radcliffe describes the discovery of the manuscript, the most significant single *action* in the book, in a kind of confused slow motion which almost reduces the very movement which makes it audible and visible to Adeline into a static tableau, a kind of Keatsian "station" which could be quite effective if it gave some subtle sign of being purposeful. When Adeline raises a bit of bedstead, it slips with a loud noise to the floor; the noise stops; silence; then she "heard a small rustling sound, and as she was about to leave the chamber, saw something falling gently among the lumber." If a reader had not become suspicious of Mrs. Radcliffe's verbal integrity, he might take "gently" as suggesting something more portentous than the word can ever denote.

The manuscript is in the usual barely legible and fragmented —which is to say "Gothic"—condition of such discoveries. Like everything else of vital significance, it suggests much more than it can say. The few words that she does read "impressed her with curiosity and terror, and induced her to return with it immediately to her chamber." While we would like her to read it immediately, we can sympathize with her unwillingness to try her sensibilities while all alone at midnight and to the ominous accompaniment of the hollow blast.

V *The Heroine's Testing in Two Worlds*

The reading is delayed so that we can return with Adeline from the imaginary horrors induced by the few words she had glimpsed to the real horrors induced by the few she can hear when, next day, she accidently but inevitably listens to a fragmented portion of a conversation between La Motte and Montalt. This is the beginning of the reciprocating terrors that batter Adeline's emotions from pillar to post, from one world to another, from dread intimations out of the past to fearful prospects of the future, from pity to terror and back again. The technical ingenuity of these counterpointed traumas is twofold: inner and outer worlds of horror provide no escape except into each other; they complement each other so that the psychological effects consequently induced by one will make the heroine more susceptible to the shocks of the other. Another stroke of ingenuity appears in retrospect when we realize that these parallel and complementary worlds are actually converging toward a single resolution which is personified in the Marquis, the initiating cause of all horrors, natural and supernatural. And, as they converge, they necessarily crush Adeline with the increasing realization (anticipated by the reader) that a single malignancy indeed directs both worlds and is preeminently concerned with establishing its ascendancy over her virtue.

Adeline continues to move about in these two worlds, veiled and only half-realized—and that half is fearful. She believes that she has heard her father mentioned, that La Motte will betray her to him. Terror is then subdued by grief at the thought that Madame La Motte, whom she had guilelessly loved, was united with her husband and the Marquis against her. She momentarily suspects human nature of being generically depraved; she is criticized briefly by the author for such a suspicion. (Later La Luc provides the expanded philosophical disquisition disproving a doctrine of man's essential evil.) She would like to read the manuscript we are all waiting for, but she is too distraught. No sooner has she composed her mind for sleep than a terrific banging announces the sudden and mysterious departure of the Marquis. Later we find he had left because of pangs of remorse or terror at the thought that in the abbey he had killed his brother. But now his action is unexplained sound and fury, as is the way with villains—abrupt, unexpected, inexplicable movements, constantly throwing quite out of joint any momentary equilibrium a heroine may deviate into.

Adeline is next day called to task for eavesdropping when she challenges La Motte about his intentions concerning her. Not only does her blush admit her awareness of her breach of etiquette, but a consequent catechism by La Motte forces her to admit that she had heard nothing at all on which to base her fears about her father. The admission is pertinent not only to fragmented sentences in a half-heard conversation but also to similar sentences in the partially legible manuscript. Radcliffean heroines are criticized in good faith by the author and others, as well as in bad faith by villains, for letting their fancy run away with the few and obscure facts they generally have at their disposal. In this instance, after having savored his moment of dialectical triumph, La Motte admits that, as a matter of fact, she had inferred correctly. He is lying; but that fact does not appear until the full brunt of fearful potential has thoroughly exercised Adeline's imagination. Mrs. Radcliffe has resorted to a familiar device for further racking Adeline's already well-stretched but fortunately resilient sensibility by giving her (and the sympathetic reader) a bare moment to hope that her worst fears are frivolous before dashing such hope with a full confirmation of La Motte's impotence, if not absolute villainy. Her protector is proved a betrayer; and Adeline resigns herself to Heaven, the last resort of defeated hopes.

Appropriately at this juncture, the Marquis returns to protest his love and to offer her his protection. We have as yet no certain grounds for despising the Marquis, nor has Adeline. She may, along with us, recall that she has been proved guilty of building nightmares on insufficient evidence; but we may also recall that, according to La Motte, she had guessed correctly. The real point of the Marquis's offer is to test Adeline's virtue in adversity when faced with a temptation which would be no temptation if the Marquis were already a proved villain. A subordinate and correlative point is to confirm Adeline's intuitions. The Marquis very soon makes it clear that his intentions are quite dishonorable. The time is now ripe for a succinct appraisal of her position, somewhere between the devil and the deep: "She threw a trembling glance upon the prospect around her. On one side was her father, whose cruelty had already been too plainly manifested; on the other, the Marquis pursuing her with insult and vicious passion" (125). And even her ostensible protector, La Motte, is a papier-mâché creation who is only strong in persecuting her.

There is only one place for Adeline to go and that is back to the room and the other world of the manuscript (and its sympathetic terror) which the room leads to. The obliterated pages of the manuscript yield little but are well filled with exclamation marks, signs of exasperation and vengeance at first, diminishing into futile impotence toward the last, but full of sensibility throughout. Because the narrative is interrupted in order for Mrs. Radcliffe to keep us suspended between the two worlds—and for Adeline to be subject to the Marquis's insulting advances and to the La Mottes' weakness or sarcastic comment—we are several pages discovering what happened to the writer. As it turns out, he had been waylaid by a band of men, clearly not bandits, who brought him to the abbey at the order of some nameless being whom, nonetheless, the writer knows and shudders at knowing. He solicits a future reader's vengeance and pity; the light in the room goes out at just this "interesting" juncture, at which little is said but much is suggested: "What a moment was that! All the thunders of Heaven seemed launched at this defenceless head! O! fortitude, nerve my heart to—" (127). Without herself mentioning names, Adeline intimates a recollection of the charges and superstitions leveled at the Marquis when she thinks of the "many attendant circumstances" that made the manuscript intriguing.

When the Marquis comes to dinner next day, a further twist is taken on the taut cord of Adeline's tortured sensibility as she is required to show him some specious courtesy because the La Mottes have told her that their safety depended on his continued goodwill. Putting disinterestedness before apprehension, she confronts the enemy as if he were a friend, even though she may be, and we certainly are, inclined to believe him the perpetrator of the manuscript atrocities, as so far intimated to us. He offers her his hand, along with an argument about self-interest which anticipates his later dialogue with La Motte: it is to Adeline's interest to marry him and protect herself. Clearly, such an appeal has no chance with her. His looks become unsupportable at dinner; she retires to the solace of her room and to the catharsis of the manuscript.

The manuscript was written by a Radcliffean who expected to find in each of several chambers he passes through an "instrument of destruction," whose diabolical mechanism and nomenclature each reader may imagine for himself. When he is simply left in prison with dire expectations for company, he offers a familiar gloss on Mrs. Radcliffe's tactics of horror: "The pang of death is, surely, not superior to that I then suffered. Shut out from day, from friends, from life—and left to imagine horrors more terrible than any, perhaps, which certainty would give—I sink beneath the . . ." (128). "Here several pages of the manuscript were decayed with damp, and totally illegible." When legibility returns, Adeline is exposed to successive blasts of sentimental pathos that emanate from a heart very much after her own sensibility.

The writer has been unjustly torn from loving friends and kin; he continues to implore sympathy from his unknown future readers: "O! ye who may hereafter read what I now write, give a tear to my sufferings; I have wept often for the distresses of my fellow-creatures!" As we might expect, Adeline responds to this direct appeal to her heart as, conceivably, we should respond to the like appeal that her distresses make to our sensibilities. As she weeps for him, so should we weep for her. As he is an ideal victim of sensibility, she is an ideal reader of his victimization. There is, in fact, little substance in the manuscript; it is a "pathetic" document intimating horrors it does not specify, much in the Radcliffean mode.

Empathy is established by a "strong illusion of fancy," and "it seemed as if his past sufferings were at this moment present." Every sentence of the narrative is an exclamation; her responses echo the emphasis and the "energy of truth" it implies: "Your miseries, O injured being! are lamented, where they were endured. *Here*, where you suffered, I weep for your suffering!" Contiguity in time rather than in space usually establishes the heroine's ability to sympathize with an absent but kindred sensibility—as Adeline can in other contexts envisage in horrible detail the sufferings and anguish of Theodore. At any rate, the passage dramatizes Adeline's disinterestedness at a time when her own prospects would seem to require all the sympathy she could muster. But, in fact, virtue is its own reward: she forgets her own miseries in lamenting another's. While we approve her moral sensibility, we are less disinterested in her fate and more inclined to recognize in these intimated horrors what she may shortly expect from the Marquis; for the villain behind the manuscript is the villain in her life. We recognize the dramatic irony of her situation as she plays out a dialogue with the writer in a soliloquy with herself. Yet we are pleased that, at the end, our inference is confirmed by the facts. And, as often, the full brunt of the irony is not revealed to us until the complicated series of revelations at the end identifies the writer as her father.

Mrs. Radcliffe works to realize the Gothic potential of the manuscript by afflicting her heroine with a hollow sigh in the wind and a phantom figure in the wings: "There was a glass before her on the table, and she feared to raise her looks toward it, lest some other face than her own should meet her eyes: other dreadful ideas, and strange images of fantastic thought crossed her mind" (129). The mirror is not a fortuitous and superficial stage prop introduced into the scene on the theory that everyone might have half-feared the same apparition under similar circumstances. Like all Radcliffean heroines, Adeline has a memory and imagination that work in concert toward the worst of horrible associations. Just before she had been handed over to La Motte, she had had a nightmare in which her supposed father presented her with a mirror in which she saw herself bleeding and heard the words she felt were "more than ideal": "Depart this house, destruction hovers here." Like the dream, the mirror is an economical Gothic device because it can obscurely shadow forth a distorted image of the world which suggests the supernatural without later requiring a conscientious author to explain away its distortions as based in nature or a distraught sensibility.

Although Adeline refuses the challenge of the mirror, she cannot escape the obscurity surrounding her. And this obscurity, working on a hypertense imagination, seems to produce "a figure, whose exact form she could not distinguish," though Mrs. Radcliffe is careful to allow this phantom a possible source in Adeline's imagination, which "refused any longer the control of reason." Next morning "her mind, soothed and invigorated by sleep, rejected the mystic and turbulent promptings of imagination." The rejection is appropriate to the good sense of the heroine, but the question remains with the reader—will it be justified in the event?

Again the Marquis, again La Motte, again the torments of a real world rush to fill a daylight void in a mind just vacated by nighttime terrors. An added spice to mystery and suspense is Peter's garrulous and unfulfilled attempt at telling Adeline something quite important. Meanwhile, Madame La Motte is evidently laboring under some great anxiety. We do not really care about her anxiety (though Adeline does), but we suppose that her worries should be Adeline's fears—were they known. Adeline puts Madame's fears and Peter's half-told tale together as substance for pensive and alarming reflection. At midnight she returns to the manuscript, whose tales are twice or trebly told without really developing beyond reiterated and inarticulate pathos. The shifting imprecision of reference and suggestion is, nonetheless, sufficient for Adeline to conclude (long after the reader had done so) that "the reports of the peasants are true. Murder has been committed." The convergence of the two worlds is, therefore, living up to our expectations, though Adeline's disinterestedness apparently keeps her from inferring the like cause behind the misery she suffers and the one she sympathizes with.

VI *The Villain*

When Peter tells her at last that La Motte is conspiring to give her to the Marquis, Adeline resolves to escape; for there is nothing wrong with escaping with a servant, who clearly has no Lovelace potential at all. The time is ripe for the ultimate castastrophe, and it occurs appropriately when her meeting with Peter is frustrated by the Marquis, who sends in Peter's stead one of his own men to carry her off to his villa. The villain's capacity for evil has been made awfully clear to us through eavesdropping and through the manuscript, but he has gained his evil stature by our inference rather than by his overt action. Until Peter's revelation, he has remained insidiously disguised behind his polished manners, behind infrequent appearances, and behind La Motte, who has played a unique role as underagent or buffer-villain.

He now emerges as an active seducer but still refrains from any open attack, either verbally or physically, on Adeline's virtue by conditioning his evil designs with music, the food of love, and with a luxurious repast decked out with near-Oriental splendor. Mrs. Radcliffe doubtless had Clarissa's actual seduction in mind (as well as *Comus*), but she would not let drugs taint the lips or intestines (much less the sensibilities) of her heroine. Music is the more subtle intoxication and, as a befuddler of the senses, is esthetically more appealing. To a responsive nature like Adeline's, it is also much more dangerous since it does actually weaken her resistance to the point where the reader is invited to fear for the outcome. But, when the Marquis asks her to choose from among the delectable and exotic fruits and viands spread in profusion before her, Adeline primly dissipates such fears, along with the heady and seductive atmosphere building up around her, by "accepting only of a peach." This test is crucial, and Adeline passes it; but we find it is difficult to judge whether Adeline, peach in hand, is insufferable or endearing. Mrs. Radcliffe's judgment is, of course, a matter of record long before the fact. The fairy-tale quality of the vignette possibly conditions the unlikelihood of Adeline's then escaping through an unlocked window, "tripping lightly along" through the moonlight and flower-bespangled lawn into the arms of an expectant Theodore, who, with a gross disregard for credibility, appears on cue to elevate the heroine from despair to momentary bliss.

Mrs. Radcliffe nowhere else evidences such deftness and particularity in mood building when the mood she creates is substantially sensual. Nowhere else is the heroine's esthetic sensibilities elicited in direct contradiction to her moral principles. And very seldom does Mrs. Radcliffe allow her heroine to shuffle and temporize, as a matter of policy and self-defense, when a villain protests his lust, as, for a bare moment, Adeline does. Directly after an editorial criticism of this hypocrisy, Adeline shakes it off. Nature and education confirm principle by disavowing policy. Yet while Mrs. Radcliffe paraphrases the moral and esthetic ingredients of *Comus*, there is really no dramatic tension because there is little dialogue to call into question Adeline's eventual triumph; contempt and displeasure in the epitomed abstract stand alone to ward off the villain's advances and to counter his protestations. Mrs. Radcliffe provides the motto for the tableau that concludes the allegory: [the Marquis] "stood for a moment the slave of virtue, though the votary of vice."

There is another test of virtue which concerns Adeline directly but which is successfully passed by La Motte, in spite of his weakness, when he decides to save rather than take her life. The most dramatic set of scenes in the novel are the two in which the Marquis plays on La Motte's self-interested fears in order to prime him for a request which surprises the reader quite as much as it shocks La Motte. We are, along with La Motte, prepared for the Marquis to ask La Motte's complicity or acquiescence in support of his designs against Adeline's honor. Since we do not know about the seal which had proved Adeline to be his niece, we do not know that, perforce, he must exchange his original designs on her chastity for the conceivably more diabolical ones on her life that he now feels necessary for his financial security.

For all La Motte's degeneracy from protector to demi-villain, he retains a moral as well as a dramatic interest for the reader because his character is weak and mixed rather than strong and evil. Unlike the Abbot in *The Sicilian Romance*, the protection he offers the heroine is not contingent on the victory of one self-interested passion over another. He is capable sporadically of a kind of grudgingly offered disinterestedness. The consecutive scenes between him and the Marquis decide Adeline's fate; and, if La Motte had been as self-interested as the Marquis thought him (and all mankind) to be, he would have served the Marquis's wicked ends. Since he rebels at this ultimate evil, even though the rebellion seems to seal his fate, he proves a contention about human nature which is later advanced by La Luc and Verneuil when they argue—in a set piece that is designedly in opposition to the Marquis's philosophy of self-interest—that human nature is indeed essentially good and achieves its greatest

pleasure in disinterested action. Though only momentarily, La
Motte experiences a glow of pleasure as he sees Adeline leave
and turns to face the consequences that the Marquis will present
him with—betrayal and imprisonment.

With the exception of a few comparable scenes in *The Italian*,
the dialogue between La Motte and the Marquis represents Mrs.
Radcliffe's best efforts at dramatizing rather than narrating an
incident crucial to her heroine and to the development of the
novel. After La Motte has confessed his criminal acts to the Marquis, he receives the latter's pity and sympathy in sentiments and
tone derived from Iago:

"Talk not of goodness," said the Marquis: "I will not pretend that
my desire of serving you is unalloyed by any degree of self-interest.
I will not affect to be more than man, and trust me those who do are
less. It is in your power to testify your gratitude, and bind me to
your interest forever." He paused. "Name but the means, name but
the means, and if they are within the compass of possibility, they
shall be executed." The Marquis was still silent. "Do you doubt my
sincerity, my lord, that you are silent? Do you fear to repose a confidence in the man whom you have already loaded with obligation?
who lives by your mercy, and almost by your means." The Marquis
looked at him, but did not speak. "I have not deserved this of you,
my lord; speak, I entreat you."

"There are certain prejudices attached to the human mind," said
the Marquis, in a slow and solemn voice, "which it requires all our
wisdom to keep from interfering with our happiness; certain set notions
acquired in infancy, and cherished involuntarily by age, which grow
up and assume a gloss so plausible, that few minds, in what is called
a civilized country, can afterwards overcome them. Truth is often
perverted by education." (163)

The argument from nature is perverted to fit his distorted perspective on the world just as much as his crimes and solicitations
have distorted the psychology of the trembling heroine. The
dramatic interlude is effective esthetically because of the innuendo that keeps in suspense the fatal request which even La
Motte cannot anticipate, though he is eager, it seems, to anticipate and assist in the deflowering of Adeline, a subject which he
supposes the Marquis is about to broach. But, like the other scenes
or tableaux, dramatized or simply presented in narration, this one
is concerned with the exposition and interplay of passions rather

than with actions. Moral sentiments, for better or for worse, are displayed in an esthetically moving context that would not be esthetic without the morality pervading it.

The dialogue of death is the dramatic counterpart to the structural coalescing of the inner and outer worlds of terror that Adeline mediates when she shuttles between the manuscript and Montalt. That is, it creates in an intensely compact dramatic situation the conditions for suspense which the intermittent manuscript reading expands over several pages and chapters. And of course it also realizes the promise intimated by the manuscript. Our worst fears had been for the life of Adeline; these fears had been suspended or replaced by our fears for her chastity. But this momentary relief—and in a world where alternatives merely distinguish degrees of evil, fears for her chastity are probably lesser fears and so a relief—only beguiles us into expecting a lesser evil until the Marquis plunges us back into the compound terrors of the manuscript intimations by unfolding his true design. Between them, the manuscript-reading sequence and this dialogue (which really climaxes it) are the structural and dramatic high points around which the rest of the novel revolves and which all pertinent incident or emotion radiates from or is attracted to. Whatever is extrinsic to these scenes—the intrusive sentimentalism of Amand's love-longing—is extrinsic to the novel. The rather tedious account of La Luc and his Happy Valley gains its dramatic justification from its moral opposition, in labored sententia and exemplum, to the Marquis's sophistic disquisitions with La Motte.

Both the Marquis and La Luc-Verneuil argue from nature to prove contrary truths about human motives and pleasures. The Marquis's nature—as his references to the untutored but noble savage (in this instance, the American Indian) indicate—is a nature red in tooth and claw, a barbarous nature in which self-interest is a paramount concern because man is still bestial. La Luc's nature is a civilized, humanized one, in which man's moral, rational, and sensitive faculties have emerged into a truly enlightened disinterestedness. The old dispensation of self-interest goes by the boards, however, when La Motte's good action denies the Marquis's sophistry. La Luc's daughter, Clara, later offers a positive confirmation of her father's essentially Hartleian position when she discovers that duty and pleasure are indeed one. Ann Radcliffe did not have to be learned to incorporate and contrast the popular moral philosophies of the day in her novel any more than she had to be especially conversant with the empirical psychology originating in Locke in order to make use of associationism for her nostalgic, sentimental, or sublime purposes. She applied popular knowledge—materials even her anticipated audience, the fair sex, would be familiar with.

VII *Technique*

Besides the *expliqué*-as-revelation which concludes the novel and a few stylistic innovations, *The Romance of the Forest* makes extended use of an expanding repertoire of technical devices meant to discriminate character or to activate the reader's suspense. Louis, as a foil in different ways to Theodore and the Marquis, represents the ideal behavior of a rejected suitor. His excruciating moral dilemma is suggested rather than emphasized, but the sensitive reader should elicit its pathos from his staunch nobility in aiding his successful rival (when he could have been indifferent to his fate) because of his love for Adeline, for Theodore, and for virtue. Unlike the Marquis and similar lovers, Louis resigns his useless protestations in order to win, at least, the esteem of his beloved. His ultimate bliss is to live close to Adeline and Theodore and to add to Adeline's social pleasures by an occasional visit.

Mrs. Radcliffe tries to parallel her relative success with La Motte by creating a mixed feminine character in his wife. The attempt is abortive and erratic and is finally forgotten about altogether as the lady moves out of the novel except for an occasional reference to her commiserating her husband's fate. The attempt at humor—made by Peter—is grotesque and contrived. The source of Mrs. Radcliffe's barren conception of dramatic humor is the Nurse in *Romeo and Juliet*, where garrulity and tediousness combine in a humorous synthesis. But Shakespeare conceived of applicable words and specific sentiments which gave life to a character and incident. About all that can be said for Mrs. Radcliffe's garrulous peasants is that they occasionally add to the suspense, which is their real technical purpose—and that purpose is often frustrated by the readers' impatience with their tediousness.

The major *expliqué* combined with revelation concerns the murdered father-brother, but we have fairly well anticipated the culprit between supernatural suggestion and unnatural action before Montalt is thoroughly exposed. And, really, there is nothing very supernatural about any of the incidents or imaginings connected with the skeleton, the dagger, the musty chambers and corridors, the secret panels, and the partially illegible manuscript. What Mrs. Radcliffe has really succeeded in depicting with this machinery is the tendency toward a belief in supernatural agencies which unnatural actions inspire in a susceptible mind. But running through the extended account of the manuscript reading and the consequent wanderings through subterraneous passageways is (a) the reader's knowledge that everything occasioning supernatural dread is the result of an unnatural act and (b) the heroine's reminders to herself and to us that the only real supernatural power is a benevolent God who, among other good acts, will cause murderers to receive their punishment in time.

Neither knowledge nor reminder keeps the reader or the heroine from reacting to the unnatural as if it were supernatural when decor and incident prescribe an involuntary suspension of rational inference. Mrs. Radcliffe's developing genius has allowed us to have our cake and eat it too: we are subconsciously aware that there is nothing supernatural about the actions and imaginings Adeline goes through; but, affirming the Coleridgean psychology of supernatural suggestion, we never let that subconscious knowledge interfere with our instinctual or esthetic sense of the supernatural possibility inherent in the heroine's surroundings. Mrs. Radcliffe has succeeded in this novel where she failed in both *Castles* and *The Sicilian Romance*: the supernatural machinery and the rhetoric of terror that sets it in motion, or is itself activated by it, are meshed with a heroine whose conventional sensibility is sufficiently demonstrated for us to sympathize with her and experience through her.

The rash of new characters which supplement the usual proliferation of incident at the end of a Radcliffean novel tend to obscure Mrs. Radcliffe's rather cumbersome attempts at explaining the major para-supernatural sequence still unresolved. La Motte's mysterious activities around the tomb had nothing to do with a tryst with Adeline, as Madame La Motte had suspected and, for a terrible moment or two, we had been tempted to believe—though, again subconsciously, we knew better. Later Mrs. Radcliffe likewise tempts us to betray our lack of faith in her representations of simon-pure virtue when, in *Udolpho*, she provides all the evidence we need to convict St. Aubert of adultery. But La Motte's visits were inspired by his morbid desire to reflect in horror over the picture of the man he had wounded—Montalt. Apparently, La Motte himself is the ghostly apparition seen at the tomb. His persistent viewing and reviewing of Montalt's pictured countenance likewise explain his blenching when Montalt first comes to the abbey. Otherwise, most of the *expliqués* in the novel are of the instant variety—we know right away that an eerie noise from the rafters is an owl or that a shadowy figure, replete with ghostly voice, is really Peter as interpreted by an overwrought imagination.

In *The Romance of the Forest*, Mrs. Radcliffe is still experimenting with the extended use of the supernatural. But she does offer abundant evidence that, on both moral and rational grounds, she will not leave her supernatural effects unexplained by natural —or rather (and more precisely)—by unnatural causes. Her value judgments are consequently implicit in her technique. The esthetic effects of supernatural suggestion are as forceful and appealing whether the agency behind them is supernatural or merely unnatural. The effects will be felt by the reader if the heroine is an appropriately compendious medium for the many passions she is supposed to feel and display. We get to know Adeline well enough to identify with her terror regardless of its inspiration— and that is all Mrs. Radcliffe wants us to do.

CHAPTER 6

The Mysteries of Udolpho

*T*HE *Mysteries of Udolpho* is the perfected synthesis of the modern and medieval romances which Walpole had prescribed and had ostensibly attempted thirty years before the publication of Mrs. Radcliffe's greatest work. All the elements of an emergent and more refined species of Gothic tale which could be discerned in *The Romance of the Forest* flourish in concert here. Amid a vast expanse of novel, the Radcliffean heroine (now called Emily) meanders leisurely through pastoral fields and Alpine mountain reaches. Or she flees in terror (when she does not swoon) through spacious halls and endless corridors as obscure and devious as the inscrutable malignancy that rules over their darkness and revels in the awful ruin environing it.

And there is Udolpho itself, the comprehensive symbol of the wrecked and somber mind permeating its turrets, ramparts, secret doors, veiled horror, isolated rooms, heavy chests, great staircases, and unlighted passageways. There are perhaps a few underdeveloped forerunners of Ann Radcliffe's rugged pile, but the dominant strain of Gothic castle evident in successive tales of terror down to the one published only yesterday can be clearly traced back to the terrific shadow hulking massive in the Apennines precisely at sunset when Emily first glimpsed its "mouldering walls of dark grey stone" and when Montoni, speaking for the first time in several hours, announced, "There is Udolpho."

I *Summary*

The story opens with the aristocratic St. Auberts and their daughter Emily living in perfect peace amid the pastoral shades and sunlight of La Vallée, their residence in the south of France. Mysterious music in the air and sonnets to Emily by an unknown admirer gently anticipate later Gothic terrors without really disturbing the idyllic calm in which Emily is educated by her father and by nature. An intrusive visit by the worldly Quesnels (Monsieur Quesnel is Madame St. Aubert's brother), who prefer the artifice of the landscape "improvers" to nature, merely enhances the virtues of the St. Auberts' way of life. Madame St. Aubert dies, and Emily and her father journey to the Pyrenees, where they soon meet the hero Valancourt, who almost immediately falls in love with Emily. Soon afterward St. Aubert dies, and Emily returns alone to La Vallée, where, according to her father's instructions, she burns (without reading them) some mysterious letters which apparently relate to the picture of a beautiful woman Emily had once seen her father view with much passion or agitation. Emily then goes to stay with her aunt in Toulouse. Valancourt follows Emily there and is granted permission to marry her, a permission which is rescinded soon after when the aunt marries the villain Montoni, who is after her (and Emily's) money, and who takes them to Venice.

After Montoni unaccountably decides against having Emily marry Count Morano (one of Montoni's villainous associates), the household leaves Venice for Udolpho, a castle high in the Apennines. The previous owner of the castle, Lady Laurentini, had mysteriously disappeared some years before. The servants claim to have seen ghosts floating about the corridors and ramparts of Udolpho. Morano appears, tries to abduct Emily, and is badly wounded by Montoni. Soon after, Montoni tries to get his wife to sign over her property to him. She refuses and he has her put in a secluded tower of the castle. Emily tries to visit her but is frightened off by some blood on the stairway which she construes to mean her aunt has been murdered by Montoni. Emily's maidservant and confidante, Annette, had told her about a mysterious room wherein was kept a mysterious veiled object which Emily herself soon visits and unveils, though she is so shocked by what she sees beneath the black veil that she tells us nothing about it. We are later told that she saw a wax image of a worm-eaten corpse which she had supposed real.

The aunt finally dies of Montoni's ill-treatment, though she is not actually murdered by him. Montoni continues his attempts to get Emily's money; Morano is foiled in another attempt to rescue or abduct her; and Montoni finally sends her away for a time. When she returns, she finds a battle had taken place at Udolpho and that an old family friend named Du Pont had been taken

prisoner by Montoni. Emily, Annette, Du Pont, and a male servant Ludovico escape Udolpho and leave Italy by boat only to be
caught in a storm which shipwrecks them on the French coast
near where Emily's father had been buried. She and her party are
rescued by the Count de Villefort and family and go to live with
them in the dilapidated château which the Villeforts had inherited
from a family named Villeroi. Emily then spends some time at
the nearby convent where her father was buried. She there discovers a nun who looks like the missing Laurentini, a portrait of
whom Emily had seen at Udolpho. Emily returns to the Villefort
château only to be frightened out of her wits by a face which
emerges from beneath a black pall on the bed of the dead mistress
of the château, whose deserted room and death chamber Emily
and a maid visited at night. Ludovico agrees to spend a night in
the chamber and is unaccountably missing at dawn. Later Villefort and his son keep the same vigil and, though they are not
spirited away, leave the room subdued and silent about what happened to them. Emily is then told by an old servant that the miniature which she had found among her father's papers was a
picture of the former Marquise de Villeroi and that Emily herself
looked very much like the picture.

Valancourt arrives at the Villefort residence but is rejected by
Emily because of the gambling and carousing he was allegedly
guilty of while he had been in Paris. Emily goes back to La Vallée to find that her lands, which Montoni had cheated her out of,
were hers once again and Montoni himself in jail. Meanwhile, the
Villeforts are waylaid by a band of outlaws while hunting in the
Pyrenees. The *expliqués* begin unraveling when their rescuer turns
out to be Ludovico, an unwilling companion of the outlaws. He
had been carried away from the room at the Villefort château by
the bandits, who had used the deserted portion of the seaside
château to store their smuggled goods. It was they who had purposely given rise to tales of ghostly noises and apparitions (including the one beneath the black pall) in order to keep the
curious away from their hideout. Emily then returns to Villefort
and to the convent where she discovers that the nun there (who
is now dying) was in reality Lady Laurentini who had left
Udolpho to be with her former lover the Marquis de Villeroi, the
original owner of the château which now belonged to the Villeforts.
She had beguiled him by her charms into poisoning his wife who

was St. Aubert's sister. And so the mystery of the miniature is explained, of St. Aubert's agitated interest in it, and its likeness to Emily, the niece of the poisoned woman, whose tragic tale St. Aubert had kept from his daughter. Both the Lady Laurentini and her lover had been overcome by remorse over their wickedness. He had died in exile, and she retired to the convent. The story comes to its happy ending when Emily marries Valancourt after discovering that he had gambled at last only to aid a friend in dire straits. They then go off to live the rest of their tranquil days at La Vallée.

Structurally speaking, the contrasted themes of sentimentality and sensationalism interpenetrate variably in the three major locales of the novel. At La Vallée Emily receives a moral and sentimental education from her father amid idyllic natural settings and pastoral associations which are increasingly imbued with Gothic overtones anticipating the sensational effects of the irrational, unnatural, and generally immoral world she will soon be forced to live in. Esthetically speaking, the movement from La Vallée to Udolpho is a movement from the world of the beautiful to the world of the sublime. Pleasurable sentiments characterize the first world; sensations of terror characterize the second. Obscurity replaces light, mystery replaces openness, Rosa replaces Poussin. The excessive sensibility which left Emily open to the positive influx of moral impulses in La Vallée leaves her open to the morally undermining effects of the unnatural environment imposed on her by Udolpho and Montoni. Though not ostensibly fit for that world by nature and education, Emily's moral sense triumphs all the more emphatically because it triumphs against the odds. The worlds of light and darkness, La Vallée and Udolpho, are joined in almost equal measure at the third major locale of the novel, Château-le-Blanc, the Villefort château. The testing of Emily's rational morality and sentimental education is here more complex, more subtle, and more stringent because the lesson she learned at Udolpho—that supernatural effects, when evil or seemingly so, stem from unnatural agents like Montoni working on a susceptible mind like Emily's—does not seem to apply. At Udolpho Emily is provided with a larger scope for esthetic and ethical reaction than a life spent at La Vallée could have given her; at Château-le-Blanc Emily learns that evil and unnatural causation can have its effects even in a world of seeming sweetness and light.

The moral implication seems to be that, if the sensibilities are strong and if the education has been proper, the unnatural phenomena which make up the Gothic world will not triumph over the heroine. Ann Radcliffe's moral tags and sporadic editorializing confirm this implication, which the incidents generally illustrate. The battle is between good and evil in the old sense as carried on by their eighteenth-century embodiments, disinterested virtue and self-interested vice. A heroine who reacts spontaneously for the right in a natural world must learn to accommodate her reactions to an unnatural one. Little wonder if at first she ascribes the unnatural phenomena around her to supernatural powers—or at least is tempted to do that. Reason and further experience will confirm innate but shaken convictions by proving at last that evil is a man-made accident which does not, in the long run, interfere with divine benevolence working through the disinterested actions of human agents. These agents will prosper sevenfold when their afflictions are done. So goes the esthetic morality of the tale.

II La Vallée: The Sentimental Education

The story begins in a context where taste and morality are the same because nature, disinterestedness, and reason maintain a gentle but effectual sway in and around the St. Aubert ménage in La Vallée:

On the pleasant banks of the Garonne, in the province of Gascony, stood, in the year 1584, the château of Monsieur St. Aubert. From its windows were seen the pastoral landscapes of Guienne and Gascony stretching along the river, gay with luxuriant woods and vine, and plantations of olives. To the south, the view was bounded by the majestic Pyrenees, whose summits veiled in clouds, or exhibiting awful forms, seen, and lost again, as the partial vapours rolled along, were sometimes frowned with forests of gloomy pine, that swept downward to their base. These tremendous precipices were contrasted by the soft green of the pastures and woods that hung upon their skirts; among whose flocks and herds and simple cottages, the eye, after having scaled the cliffs above, delighted to repose. To the north, and to the east, the plains of Guienne and Languedoc were lost in the mist of distance: on the west, Gascony was bounded by the waters of Biscay. (223)

The figures gradually come to life out of their pastoral background to express sentiments akin to their time of life, with Aubert settling into the deserved quiescence of old age and Emily informing her mind with his precepts and with nature's beauty.

The picturesque nature surrounding the Aubert dwelling emphasizes beauty rather than sublimity, with a sense of idyllic unreality distancing not only the "bold precipices of the Pyrenees" but even the human inhabitants, who appear as groups or figures in Mrs. Radcliffe's verbal painting. Emily and her father "wandered away among the most romantic and magnificent scenes, nor suffered the charms of Nature's lowly children to abstract them from the observance of her stupendous works." The cabin of the shepherd, the peasant dance, the izard that bounds among the rocks are alike still lifes, with nothing specific coming to the fore but with everything flowing statically through paragraph after paragraph like the meandering Garonne River which flows through the scenery with no perceptible movement: "The peasants of this gay climate were often seen on an evening, when the day's labour was done, dancing in groups on the margin of the river. Their sprightly melodies, *débonnaire* steps, the fanciful figure of their dances, with the tasteful and capricious manner in which the girls adjusted their simple dress, gave a character to the scene entirely French" (224).

Emily's keenly wrought sensibility is likewise requisite for catching the intimations of word or look—or simply something electric and sublime which floats between her and Valancourt to integrate their minds and hearts. Valancourt "often dropped suddenly from the most animating vivacity into fits of deep musing; and there was sometimes an unaffected melancholy in his smile, which Emily could not avoid understanding, for her heart was interested in the sentiment it spoke."

The feeling, as always, gives the action its importance, or, where there is no action to speak of, replaces it. St. Aubert's dangerous sickness is simply a prelude to the pastoral scene which celebrates his initial recovery and is an occasion, meanwhile, for some intermittent fears, tears, and suspense. Tangential threats of banditti, a way occasionally lost, even the mysterious château and its prophetic music never emerge into descriptive or dramatic existence of their own in these early pages. They are psychological events whose existence is contingent on the degree of response they evoke in those whose experience they pass through. The novel, through its first fifty thousand words or so, could have little interest for those superficial readers and critics whom Johnson had criticized long ago as interested in the mere story rather than in its pathos. The high point of sentimental disinterestedness is reached not when Valancourt prances about in joy at having emptied his purse to aid a destitute family but when he gives up his sleeping room to a mule.

St. Aubert's deathbed advice to Emily, which is mainly a warning (with appropriate qualification) against the sensibility which she inherits from him, deserves extensive quotation because it provides the guidelines by which Emily's future conduct should be understood and judged:

"Above all, my dear Emily," said he, "do not indulge in the pride of fine feeling, the romantic error of amiable minds. Those who really possess sensibility ought early to be taught that it is a dangerous quality, which is continually extracting the excess of misery or delight from every surrounding circumstance. And since, in our passage through this world, painful circumstances occur more frequently than pleasing ones, and since our sense of evil is, I fear, more acute than our sense of good, we become the victims of our feelings, unless we can in some degree command them. . . . I know you will say that you are contented sometimes to suffer, rather than give up your refined sense of happiness at others; but when your mind has been long harassed by vicissitude, you will be content to rest, and you will then recover from your delusion: you will perceive that the phantom of happiness is exchanged for the substance; for happiness arises in a state of peace, not of tumult: it is of a temperate and uniform nature, and can no more exist in a heart that is continually alive to minute circumstance, than in one that is dead to feeling. You see, my dear, that though I would guard you against the dangers of sensibility, I am not an advocate for apathy." (259)

These final words before Emily enters a world of stress and terror are appropriate enough, coming as they do from her preceptor as well as father. But their real purpose is to condition the reader to expect Emily to do precisely what she does do as she extracts the excess of misery from surrounding circumstance. Victims of sensibility were common enough during the eighteenth century, but few of them suffered from outer circumstances which were objectively as oppressive as those Emily passes through. Nonetheless, they are seldom really as bad as she feels them to be. The moral purpose of the *expliqués* and revelations which rationalize supernatural fears away into the trivia of daily occurrence—or at any rate into naturally explicable occurrence—is simply that they prove that Emily's refined sensibility has extracted more from the circumstances than they warrant. Such a reaction is, of course, quite as it should be from the esthetic point of view. Emily is a sentimental heroine only because she fulfills her father's fears before she gains the peace of mind he hopes for her. And it is also true that, without her exquisite sensibility, she would not be able to respond to the sublimity of the landscape which elevates her above persecution, much less to the largely tacit love of Valancourt.

III *Udolpho: The Trial by Terror*

Examples of disinterestedness and esthetic sensibility proliferate until St. Aubert dies and Emily passes into the world of unnatural experience, or the world dominated by archexemplars of self-interest. The St. Aubert château is contrasted with Montoni's castle as are the characters and environments within and around them; they play out their contrasting roles in the sensibility of the heroine who lives through both of them. The picturesque setting of the St. Aubert château emphasizes the beautiful and the pastoral rather than the starkly terrible sublime. Instead of encroaching precipices combining with the gloomy front of a moldering castle, *chez* Aubert is redolent of "pleasant banks," "pastoral landscapes," "luxuriant woods and vine and plantations of olives." For pictorial contrast, but at an appropriately esthetic distance, appear the "tremendous precipices," "frowning forests of gloomy pine" which the "eye . . . scaled" before returning to the Claudean "flocks, herds, and simple cottages" where it "delighted to repose." At Udolpho, the decor is reversed. While the immediate approaches to Udolpho are not consistently dismal, "shaggy inacessible steeps" and a vista exhibiting the "Apennines in their darkest horror" effectively condition Emily for the castle and the "gloomy silence" of Montoni himself.

Emily's shining sensibility, a little spot of La Vallée in the midst of Udolpho's horror, is contrasted both to Montoni's gloomy disposition and to the dully reflective surface of her maid Annette's rather meager responsive apparatus. Montoni is immune to pronounced Gothic suggestion (the voice from nowhere which ominously echoes his words), while Annette would see a phantom in every candle flicker. Montoni is dreadfully silent in his omnipotence, whereas Annette is only too willing to confuse Emily's already-confused conjectures with garrulous spates of misinformation. Or, if Annette has stumbled over a fragment of truth, Emily's unwillingness to tamper with a servant's integrity keeps her from taking advantage of Annette's clear willingness to tell all she knows.

Montoni gradually emerges from his first appearance as a polished, rather attractive middle-aged man at a social function into the husband of Madame Montoni and thence to his significant role as Emily's victimizer. His actual atrocities are generally implied rather than carried out. His character is by now stereotyped by its precedents in Montalt, Mazzini, and Malcolm. He shows his power not so much in his actions toward Emily as in his relations with his wife and with his fellow villains. Each subordinate villain is capable of a good deal of evil in his own right. But their major function is, collectively, to enhance Montoni's villainous character by inevitably giving in to his superior will. As they argue among themselves, with words or knives, he sits apart in silence until at the crucial moment he orders or acts; and their violence is then subdued to his authority. The most staunch among them, the suitor-villain Morano, is relatively well realized as a strong, ingenious, and audacious opponent to Montoni, so that Montoni can gain the greater glory or infamy in his villainy by outwitting Morano's ingenuity and by physically quelling both his strength and audacity.

Montoni's imprisonment of his wife is the worst of his consummated evils. It initiates the most expansive and detailed Gothic incident at Udolpho, one which concludes with a double frustration for both Emily and Morano. Before Montoni sent his wife to the east turret, Emily had already indicated that she felt no malice toward her spiteful aunt. Once imprisoned, she becomes an object of Emily's disinterested concern. "Like an angel of light encompassed by fiends" and occasionally "pursued by images of horror," she makes several sorties through darkened halls toward the east turret and the aunt she now presumes dead. Montoni tells her that "she has been taken care of."

Intermittently she has time to return to the many horrors oppressing her—Montoni, the ruffians about the castle, the mysterious occupant of a nearby room, the Black Veil—and to heighten these horrors by contrast, she is allowed to think of her home and parents. Even the natural phenomena are presented in quiet contrast to the tumult which agitates all the inhabitants of the castle. She thinks of departed souls. She hears mysterious music. Her state of mind is conditioned for whatever horrors may follow: "human reason cannot establish her laws on subjects lost in the obscurity of the imagination, any more than the eye can ascertain the form of objects that only glimmer through the dimness of night." The parallel is peculiarly apt to a Gothic epistemology where only shadowy objects of vision are presented to reason on their way toward the imagination, where they are interpreted according to the fears they arouse.

When the porter Bernardine tells Emily he must see her at dusk in order to impart certain grave matters that much concern her, she goes, with fearful expectation, to meet him on the rampart, while Montoni and his underdemons can be heard carousing below. Here, as often, Mrs. Radcliffe makes use of her favorite scene from *Hamlet*, or one of the two main scenes in which the ghost appears. She was doubtless aware of her readers' associations and what they would expect to appear from the dusk at the next clock beat. After Bernardine utters a series of ambiguous remarks heavily weighted to suggest the aunt is dead, he finally says that she is alive and that he will lead Emily to her. Emily then suspects that it is she herself that Montoni is going to kill. She then blames herself for letting her "romantic imagination" carry her away from probability. But she catches a look of "malignant triumph" on Bernardine's face. We are given to understand that Annette apparently knows where Bernardine is taking her and that it is not to the aunt; and we may well conjecture (since Annette is faithful to Emily, according to her comprehension) that, for all his rough exterior, Bernardine is bent on an angelic mission. He will deliver Emily to Valancourt. He does not; he delivers her to Morano, but Montoni prevents the abduction.

Since the surprise is one of the best managed in Mrs. Radcliffe's works, it is worth inspecting more closely to see how the author led up to it without our anticipations diluting its effect. There was only one brief parenthetical aside which told us that Morano—whom Montoni had seriously wounded when he had attempted to abduct Emily—was alive and well in Venice. Indifferent news it seemed at the time and easily obscured by the immediacy of Bernardine's hulking malignancy. Our tendency to trace all evil to Montoni abets the misconception which Emily introduces. The obvious question we fail to ask is why Montoni should go to so much trouble to get Emily murdered when he has already clarified his power to us and to Emily as absolute. He need not send Bernardine with secret messages which eventuate in a secret meeting which leads to a series of vaults and corridors (there is even—in anticipation of the mock-horror castle of the amusement park—a corpse glimpsed under a veil in one passageway) which leads to a graveyard. This course is the usual one for a Gothic heroine to take on her way to an escape, but such underhanded means to his murderous end are hardly required by a villain who can perpetrate his crimes with impunity in the unnatural world he has miscreated.

One reason we do not question Emily's half-inference is that she herself directs our attention away from the sort of consideration her suspicions could elicit from us when she admits that her rapid flights of imagination had gone quite beyond the realm of probability. The self-criticism, as often, is likely to be inverted by the reader. What Emily discountenances we continue to consider as a likelihood simply because she discountenances it. What she really does is to call our attention to a red herring which Mrs. Radcliffe provides to throw us off the scent of a speculative chase that might forestall her surprise by our ferreting out Morano before she springs him on us. Mrs. Radcliffe strongly flavors the herring when she has Emily remind herself that, if Madame Montoni is dead, then only Emily stands in the way of Montoni's succeeding to the money he has expended his time and fury on throughout much of the book. Emily cannot suffer herself to believe her uncle would be guilty of so despicable a crime; but since we have been more or less accustomed to suppose that Emily is meant to be his victim eventually, we are less likely to share her qualified estimate of Montoni's depravity. The reasons which Emily adduces to discard are precisely the reasons that keep Montoni in the forefront of our suspicions. If Emily had been less rational and discriminating in adducing and discarding, we might have ourselves precluded Montoni and looked elsewhere for a culprit. The looming fact of Bernardine's secrecy and his malignant looks could have led us to the simple truth which would have indicated Morano before the fact of his appearance.

Annette's apparent complicity in the conspiracy may lead us to doubt Montoni's part in the escape. But it then misleads us in the other direction: we suppose bliss rather than misery, as we expect young Valancourt to come riding. But once we know the truth, we recognize that Annette's actions and givings out were in keeping with her relative values and her apparent estimate of her mistress's true feelings. Surely Morano is better than Montoni. But, according to conventional standards we may accept for the sake of being at one with Emily, the single fate worse than death is a successful ravisher. When Morano appears on the scene, he not only surprises us by his appearance but also adds Gothic substance to our surprise by providing us with an eventuality more horrible than were those wild imaginings we had shared with Emily even after she had disowned them. And we should note, too, that we could have kept a corner of our imagination free for the pretended motive of the midnight tryst and the consequent furtive wanderings about the corridors and vaults of the castle without diminishing our overall sense of horror at the anticipated outcome of Emily's adventure. Not until Mrs. Radcliffe has let us suffer through and relish the host of alternatives, good (only one) and bad, she more than recompenses our defeated expectations with the appearance of Morano from the web of misleading conjecture in which she had successfully hidden him.

Emily's genius for misreading obscure innuendo aggravates her sensibility when she finally does visit the east turret (Mrs. Radcliffe has not denied us the horrors of the turret; only delayed them). She has supposed Montoni to intimate his wife's death. The hollow voice greeting Emily's entrance to the turret can therefore be construed as a ghost's until she discovers that it emanates from the pale and emaciated—but living—face of Madame Montoni. A short series of *expliqués* diminish into the natural order of things a few of the previous assaults on her sensibility: a track of blood, which had apparently intimated to her the death of Madame, belonged to a soldier who had been wounded in battle; and the corpse which had "confirmed Emily's horrible suspicion" belonged to another man who had fallen in the same fray.

It may be noted parenthetically that small wars and the rumors of such wars are a constant background to the trials of Emily, but they are never considered significant enough for detailed consideration. Possibly their most important function is to convert Montoni into the leader of a group of officially tolerated banditti who are allowed to selectively pillage the countryside in recompense for an occasional service they may render to the government in time of war. All of this outer bustle merely aids to condition Emily for inner affrights of the sort Mrs. Radcliffe seems gently to chide when she notes that, "had her terror permitted her to persevere longer [in calling to Madame Montoni on an earlier visit to the turret], she would probably have awakened Madame Montoni, and have been spared much suffering." Mrs. Radcliffe cannot resist letting us relish in retrospect the dramatic irony of Emily's insufficiently sustained calling powers—nor would she have cared to spare us the terrors Emily consequently endured.

In the affair of the black veil, which shall be discussed later in this chapter, Emily is likewise too terrified to probe an apparent ghostly phenomenon to its natural (or unnatural) cause. In such cases Emily's esthetic sensibility is tested to the breaking point. She shrieks, runs, or faints, though it should be noted that when a moral issue is in question Emily transcends her fears to do the right thing. Her moral education at La Vallée proves sufficient to overcome the unnatural horrors of Udolpho, and, whether Montoni knows it or not, when Emily flees his castle she has fairly well defeated his designs and proved the superiority of virtue over vice by her disinterested actions. The psychological warfare that had been waged in her mind between imagination and reason is likewise resolved in favor of reason, but not before her fancy had helped the reader to share to the full the potential for horror implicit in every darkened passageway and ghostly utterance.

IV *Château-le-Blanc: The Final Test*

When Emily arrives at the Villefort château and looks back at the supposed supernatural experiences at Udolpho that had so much terrified her, she seems almost to patronize the superstitious young girl she had then been. "I perceive," she says ("smiling") when told of ghosts at Château-le-Blanc, "that all old mansions are haunted; I am lately come from a place of wonders; but unluckily since I left it, I have heard almost all of them explained." Though Emily, we're told, was really more inclined to believe in these wonders than she here suggests, her hubris is fairly well established by her words, and we may be assured that nemesis—in the form of something ghostly or bloody—will find a way to plague her even in the well-ordered confines of a château where villains seem entirely lacking. She has faced and triumphed over supposed supernatural phenomena in the unnatural environment of Udolpho. She will now be faced with comparable phenomena in an environment like La Vallée, where it is not at all clear to her or to the reader that there is anywhere an unnatural or wicked cause to explain them away. The mystery is therefore more complex and the temptation to terror and superstition even greater than it was when Montoni was on the scene to motivate these irrational fears in the heroine's mind.

One of Mrs. Radcliffe's anonymous chapter epigraphs cryptically sums up her narrative technique: "A surprise—an adventure—a mystery." The best of the Gothic adventures in the novel is the progress through the darkened halls of the Villefort château to the chamber in which the Marchioness de Villeroi had died some twenty years before. Each step taken by Emily and by the servant Dorothea is full of prickly sensations for them and the reader. The accumulated incidents building up, detail on detail, to the lifting of the black pall on the Marchioness's deathbed are even more subtly and effectively manipulated in the direction of absolute terror than the Gothic discoveries of *The Romance of the Forest* or the Bernardine episode at Udolpho. But the technique is the same—eternal suspense spiced with tidbits of horrible suggestion leading to a climactic moment when the face appears from beneath the pall and the ladies run screaming from the room. The consequent *expliqué*—that the ghost was only a smuggler—does nothing at all to alleviate the original terror that Emily and her reader suffered.

The most surprising mystery of the novel is Ludovico's disappearance from the same chamber. While the *expliqué* again seems contrived when it comes about, the mystery had been well perpetrated and established not only by the disappearance itself but also by the enveloping context of ghostly speculation which is carried on by the Count de Villefort and the Baron St. Foix. When, after several days, Ludovico is still missing, the Count and his son decide to spend a night in the same chamber. The Count continues to discountenance supernatural phenomena, spends the night there, and emerges a chastened man. But he refuses to say what happened; and, excerpting from *Hamlet*, with ominous association, he asks the Baron neither to ask him about it nor to comment on "everything remarkable you may observe in my conduct" toward his family. To Emily, he is both plainer and more ambiguous; he tells her not to believe in the ghostly fantasies she hears from "my lady abbess," but he then concludes with a profound sigh, "the apparition of the dead comes not on light or sportive errands to terrify or to surprise the timid." So we are left with this mystery suspended and unrationalized until Ludovico appears much later to aid Blanche and St. Foix in their escape from the bandits who had spirited him away.

Nonetheless, we are not left in doubt regarding Mrs. Radcliffe's opinion. In editorializing her commentary into the text, she warns the reader (and the critic) against expecting their supernatural fancies to be realized:

On the disappearing of Ludovico, Baron Saint Foix seemed strengthened in all his former opinions concerning the probability of apparitions, though it was difficult to discover what connexion there could possibly be between the two subjects, or to account for this effect, otherwise than by supposing that the mystery attending Ludovico, by exciting awe and curiosity, reduced the mind to a state of sensibility which rendered it more liable to the influence of superstition in general. It is, however, certain that from this period the baron and his adherents became more bigoted in their own systems than before, while the terrors of the count's servants increased to an excess that occasioned many of them to quit the mansion. . . . (477)

In one view, Mrs. Radcliffe is guilty of a kind of pompous teasing or, worse, of hypocritical sententiousness. After all, she does want us to feel to the full the supernatural effects she has gone to so much trouble to induce in us. But it is also true that she is speaking partly as the rational intelligence of the novel as opposed to the superstitious and irrational elements that set it off. That is, in a given circumstance Emily would say the same thing; the Count does say it. This intelligence, coming from author or character, does not really prevent the reader from speculating beyond its limits; but it does provide the firm moral and rational base upon which Mrs. Radcliffe builds her *expliqué*. She can say, to all our frustrated hopes for a real ghost, that she had explicitly led us to the opposed conclusion, however much the empirical evidence had misled us away from it. And it misled us because our minds had been excited to awe and curiosity, and we are therefore more liable to the influence of superstition in general.

On another level of inner tension, we esthetically desire a supernatural conclusion, though our moral sensibility pronounces against it. Ideally, as Mrs. Radcliffe has said, our esthetic sense would conform with our moral sense if it were functioning decorously. Practically speaking, the effect of her art depends on our sensibilities being so thrown out of order and so distorted that we accept the misconceptions that Emily entertains. The point is, there is no incongruity between a mind or sensibility reacting differently at different times and under different circumstances. Along with Emily, we can vacillate from reason to superstitious dread without essential contradiction. Our vacillations are contingent on circumstances and upon the delicacy or perhaps vigor of our sensibilities.

Criticism of such vacillation and the kind of sensibility it implies comes from Emily herself, from Mrs. Radcliffe, from good folk like St. Aubert and Villefort, and from bad folk like Montoni, his wife, and Morano. The criticisms of the bad folk stem from uncomprehending insensibility or self-justifying motives and are only ironic confirmation of their ability to distort relevant sentimental scripture to suit their purposes. The criticisms of Emily (and of the others) are those of a disproportion (rather than distortion) of the heroine's outlook and, more painfully, her inlook. She has to adjust a sanguine view of human nature to fit the facts of life without losing her sensibility, her faith, her hopes, and her mind. But an excess of sensibility responding to a distorted world of fact—that is, Montoni's distorted world is still a fact of the heroine's life—leads to fanciful inferences which blend in fairly well with contextual terrors, subversive of reason, nature, and morality; and thereby they gain a reality to the heroine's imagination which overwhelms customary controls. When reason returns, the heroine criticizes herself for having let it escape.

There are two opposed inferences from Emily's (and others') strictures on her vacillating sensibility, both of which are justifiable according to the opposition between rational prescript and esthetic practice in Mrs. Radcliffe's novels. It is true that imagination customarily carries the heroine beyond the bounds of probability in visualizing dire events; it is also true that the actual event is often as unlikely as those which do not occur. In the world she is made to live in, only the unnatural and unlikely are worth considering because immediate causation in this world is immoral, unnatural, and irrational. Still, the heroine could save herself some terror pangs if she would restrain her imagination.

In fact, a Radcliffean heroine sporadically realizes that the best thing for her to do is to give up reflecting on the past and projecting into the future. Reflections on past bliss only aggravate present misery. She has no control over her future, so far as action is concerned. But she can at any rate make the present tolerable by refusing to imagine the variety of evils this uncontrollable future may hold in store for her. That is the strong implication of both editorial comment and self-criticism. Repeated occurrences of the improbable do not justify the heroine's imaginative flights if such flights conflict with an ultimate assurance in a rational beneficence that orders the moral as well as metaphysical universe. But, in esthetic practice, if Emily did that—if she grounded her flights—she would considerably diminish the dramatic impact of those paragraphs full of alternative horrors in which she immerses her sensibility.

The Radcliffean heroine takes shape and gains whatever character she has because of the tensions between her esthetic and ethical reactions to whatever world she finds herself in. The esthetic and the ethical are fairly well identified in La Vallée; they are opposed at Udolpho; and they are mixed at the Villefort château. But though the mixture provides Emily with her hardest tests, it is for that reason calculated to give her her last best triumph over misinferences in both the metaphysical and moral spheres. Ludovico is found, and Valancourt is redeemed. Reason and natural morality are justified. The apparent supernatural and apparent immoral ingredients in both mysteries—since Valancourt's immorality is enigmatic, given his good nature—turn out to be the effects of unnatural agencies or evil circumstances. Emily's principles, metaphysical and moral alike, are established at La Vallée, opposed at Udolpho, and finally confirmed at Villefort.

V   *Unimaginable Horrors*

Two of the most celebrated mysteries in *Udolpho* elicit a book full of suspense from the reader before they dwindle into the aftermaths of the novel's two most questionable *expliqués* or revelations: the mystery of the letters which Emily must burn without reading, and the mystery of the black veil behind which Emily does indeed look—but does not speak of. Both mysteries are intensified because Emily sees and reveals just enough for us to imagine abominations which are worse than the reality, though perhaps not much worse. Although our confidence in our moral discrimination and our rational powers is shaken, Mrs. Radcliffe's technical virtuosity is called into question in both instances, along with her artistic integrity. Why, after all, did she fail to tell us what Emily saw in the letters and behind the veil? Since throughout the novel we are given Emily's perspective on her world, we feel cheated when, for the sake of exciting our morbid speculations or sensational inferences, the author lets Emily glimpse a set of dreadful words we never see and lift a veil on an unknown object that remains unrevealed to us. When the truth dribbles out at the end, we may, along with Emily, smile at our doubts and fears; or we may disengage ourselves (on our own this time) from Emily's perspective and accuse Mrs. Radcliffe of cheating and even misleading our expectations.

The simple but cheap justification is that Mrs. Radcliffe wants us in suspense regardless of the means it takes to get and keep us there. More subtly, she is titillating our capacity for misreading shadowy evidence so that we imagine the worst in spite of our better judgment. Our moral judgment is first misled—and willfully misled—by Mrs. Radcliffe when she strongly reiterates the possibility that the words which Emily saw in the papers she had burned intimated a liaison between St. Aubert and the "other woman." Eventually, we are misled into believing that this other woman was the Marchioness de Villeroi. On no less or greater authority than the lurid and deranged imagination of Laurentini, we infer that Emily is the product of that liaison. The moral consequences of this series of inferences from shady evidence are, of course, absolutely destructive of the image of St. Aubert which all the clear evidence of the novel had so far built for us.

Mrs. Radcliffe neatly and chastely avoids spelling out the inferences we make until the truth has restored order to our moral universe. She then admits that even Emily was not so certain as she should have been about her father's premarital relations. Depending on our degree of concern or identification with Emily's moral inferences, we may feel relieved or surprised that she shared our suspicions. The revelation of the Villeroi-Laurentini liaison is horrid enough, particularly when it is enhanced by the Marchioness's murder. But it is horrid offstage, and it is "naturally" so because the whole affair is the product of unnatural passions and consequent actions. The intolerably horrid conclusion would have been the immoral and unnatural liaison we have been led to suspect. Mrs. Radcliffe succeeds in thrilling us through and through with the possibility of such a liaison which, had it existed, would have caused the engaged reader to give up moral questions in despair and to become as misanthropic as an Adeline is tempted to become in *The Romance of the Forest*.

Clearly, such an outcome to her probings would have quite shattered Emily's moral sensibility. The fact that she is not allowed to admit to herself and to us the subliminal suspicions that strong but misleading evidence arouse in her signifies Mrs. Radcliffe's unwillingness to plague her heroine's conscious thought with an image which might irremediably taint it or suggest a lack of moral faith behind it.

The handling of the incident also provides a parallel to Emily's refusal to tell us what she saw behind the black veil and a justification for Mrs. Radcliffe's willingness to tolerate and even abet her silence. Emily's horror at what she saw—or thought she saw—rendered her not only speechless but also "thoughtless" and imageless immediately after the event itself. Since our concern—and Mrs. Radcliffe's—is primarily with reactions on the heroine's imagination and sensibility, rather than with actions or the merely empirical sense of things, we are fittingly presented with the blank sense of imageless horror which Emily's conscious mind refuses to admit in any detail. She cannot admit her father's liaison because it would destroy or considerably weaken her moral principles; she cannot image to herself the horror that she saw because it would destroy her mind—and Emily, we are told on occasion, comes close to losing her mind when dire circumstance closes in on every side.

Mrs. Radcliffe is not bound to admit to us what Emily will not admit to herself. The perspective we have from Emily's mind—not from her *eye* necessarily—may present us with a universal blank which appropriately indicates the absolute horror which the fearful obscurity she generally moves in is constantly approaching.

The tacit appeal to our imaginations, in all their infinitely extravagant potential, is similar to the recurrent abdication of her descriptive task Mrs. Radcliffe is guilty of when she tells us a scene, event, or reaction may be "more easily imagined than expressed." But Emily really imagines nothing definitively. And we are therefore given a precise description of her reaction when we are given nothing but the fact of its ineffability.

Notice is given in the text that Emily really has no clear idea about what she is reacting to when she implies that she knows something more dire about the black veil than Annette has been told. She even intimates at times that she feels whatever she has seen will escape its room and attack her. Since what she thinks she has seen is a worm-eaten corpse, we must suppose that her reason has been so affected that she has given in to the grossest superstitions. And in such a state of mind whatever memory she has of the incident must be irrational and unsure. She does not verbalize what fragments of sense she might have culled from the letters she burned because the ordering of her suspicions into words would have been too much for her moral sensibility. The reader is supposed to infer from that silence and from this one that, as a matter of psychological self-preservation, Emily simply cannot tell us what she does not want to know. What Mrs. Radcliffe may be trying to give us is a kind of wordless metaphor for the defensive vacuum her heroine's mind sustains itself in (and with) in a state of shock. Emily's silence is therefore a legitimate rhetorical gesture illustrating a state of mind so delicately balanced in its own confusion that the words which would truly clarify for it what the lady thought she saw would bring it tumbling down. Through St. Aubert, Mrs. Radcliffe has warned Emily and the reader that her excessive sensibility is quite capable, when wrought upon, of misconstruing facts to suit its morbid and self-aggravating fancy. Emily's genius for misconstruction has gone about as far as it can go when it exits into silence.

Amid the usual spate of inconsequential *expliqués* that conclude her novels, Mrs. Radcliffe tells us what Emily's fancy had constructed behind the verbal blackout she presented the reader with. She thought the corpse was Laurentini's and that Montoni had murdered her and left her to rot. How seriously one should take this explanation as one which actually occurred to either Emily or Mrs. Radcliffe when the black veil was lifted is debatable. Mrs. Radcliffe's *expliqués* are usually manifest afterthoughts. But if we do care to take it seriously, it does in itself supply sufficient motive for Emily's unwillingness to admit in words or image to herself the horrible implications of such a crime, which would thereby serve as a precedent for the murder of her aunt and herself. More likely, we may assume that there is one Mrs. Radcliffe at work in the midst of Emily's confrontation with the unimaginable horror behind the veil and another at work during the process of rationalizing it away. The real—or at any rate the esthetically interesting—Mrs. Radcliffe is the first one, the one who knows and writes that "human reason cannot establish her laws on subjects lost in the obscurity of the imagination, any more than the eye can ascertain the form of objects that only glimmer through the dimness of night." The second Mrs. Radcliffe is the prim moralist about her official business of tidying up and airing out her chamber of horrors by letting in the dry light of reason and common day.

Mrs. Radcliffe seldom obtrudes unbearable horrors on her heroines. When she does, they faint or scurry by in a half-perceiving dream. Her moral and artistic sense combined to eliminate "hardcore horror" because it was unwholesome, unseemly, and relatively ineffectual. Adeline does not stumble over the skeleton of her father, as we may hope or fear, but on the dagger which may have killed him; for certain things exist which a heroine should not and need not be exposed to. In the rare instance that such exposure is allowed, the reaction is an appropriately compounded shock which may even be beyond remedying by the usual antidote, fainting. A superrefined sensibility is simply shocked out of its wits and of all articulate speech when some unimaginable visual or tactile impression is conveyed to its exceptionally low threshold of terror-trauma.

A little before Emily and the rest move back into the Claudean pastoral landscape they had emerged from at the beginning of the novel, she implies the moral of the story so far as it concerns supernatural phenomena. She has been told that the face she had seen behind the black pall was the face of a hidden bandit: "Emily could not forbear smiling at this explanation of the deception which had given her so much superstitious terror, and was surprised that she could have suffered herself to be thus alarmed, till she considered that, when the mind has once begun to yield to the weakness of superstition, trifles impress with the force of conviction" (510). We may smile along with her; but, with *Udolpho* in mind, we may hesitate to disallow a future set of similar phenomena which may dissipate the smiles and require a more penetrating analysis than the mysteries of either Udolpho or Villefort required. All we need do is yield once to the force of superstition—and Mrs. Radcliffe provides us with every incentive to yield.

The basic moral conflict between self-interest and disinterest grounds the metaphysical conflict between the supernatural and the natural. But, while Emily's esthetic sensibility wavers itself and sometimes staggers her reason, her morality remains firmly based in disinterested action. Selfish fears of the supernatural, or like unnatural horrors, are merely esthetic concerns; and they are banished when an appeal to basic ethical principle is made and consequent action called for. The reader is allowed to share the esthetic vacillation—and he is thereby entertained—with no real fear that his heroine's moral sensibility will be corrupted or cal-loused by the trials she endures; and that assurance is confirmed by the moral lesson finally delivered.

Again, there is no development of character as growth or actual mutation of character. There is simply an exposé of moral char-acter in situations where it is tested by experiences which the esthetic sensibility responds to, is shaken by, and even gives in to. The moral sensibility never gives in, but it feels the esthetic stress applied to its principles. The reason "excessive sensibility" is dan-gerous is that it could, in a nature less firmly grounded than Emily's, subvert the morality of the individual while rendering his life miserable in the esthetic view. Adeline, more than Emily, is tempted to give in to misanthropy. But then she is exposed almost exclusively to self-interest and betrayal through much of the novel.

It should be clear that, by introducing the supernatural into the sentimental novel, Mrs. Radcliffe was able to expand the range of her heroine's esthetic testing without really risking her moral triumph. There were, of course, true victims of sensibility in the sentimental novel; but Mrs. Radcliffe's sense of poetic or senti-mental justice required that virtue remain intact and triumphant throughout. On the other hand, she was able to achieve a larger range in which unnatural and self-interested action could fail. What she lost, at least for modern readers, was human characters.

She seemed willing to make the sacrifice on the assumption, it seems, that semiallegorical figures would serve to convey the dramatic passions (not actions) that she felt her readers were really interested in reading about and sharing in. Again, Johnson's comment about these superficial readers who read for mere story, is the apropos eighteenth-century justification of her assumption.

The heroine's relatively rational superstitions are intermediate between the callous disregard for the supernatural evidenced by the villain and the ready assumption of it which the servants and peasants allow themselves. After all rational and empirical interpretations have been exhausted, after terror variously inspired has disrupted her faculties, the heroine surrenders to superstition. As rational characters like Villefort indicate, it would be wrong not to allow for supernatural intervention in a good cause. Comparable aberrations from usual strictures on belief and feeling are evidenced by St. Aubert who, in spite of his stoic philosophy, weeps when his wife dies and even afterward when natural associations recall her memory; and by Emily's continued love for Valancourt, despite her recognition of his moral shortcomings. Nature emergent in the late eighteenth century was nature triumphant, though fortunately reason and decorum finally confirm nature as they are confirmed by it.

CHAPTER 7

The Italian

*T*HE *Mysteries of Udolpho* probably deserves its status as the greatest of Mrs. Radcliffe's novels. It is certainly the most representative of her works, and it is possibly the one Gothic novel a reader should be familiar with if he has only the time and inclination for reading one. The classic Gothic incidents, the highly sensitized heroine, and the abundant nature descriptions are the major features that justify its reputation. But no one since Catherine Morland has ever wished it to be any longer: it is diffuse, redundant, and it incessantly exposes the reader to the same suspense, the same nature, and the same transparent heroine.

The Italian is probably Mrs. Radcliffe's best novel because it is consistently the most interesting. And it is most interesting because the title-villain Schedoni is the only successful character creation in Mrs. Radcliffe's works. There is also a resurgence of the hero, who, while suffering some in comparison with the villain, plays a larger part in the action of the novel than either of his significant predecessors, Theodore and Valancourt. However, the role of the heroine Ellena is consequently diminished. But the result of her diminished role is the creation of a due proportion among the major characters of a novel which delivers hero and villain alike from their routine assignments elsewhere as mere sounding boards or stimuli for her sensibility. Another happy consequence of her withdrawal from stage center on occasion is that the novelist is then able to present a greater variety of action and reaction than takes place in any of the other novels.

I *Summary*

In the story—set in Naples, Italy around 1760—the hero, Vincentio di Vivaldi, hears Ellena di Rosalba singing in church. Generally impressed by what he hears and later sees, he finds occasion to make her acquaintance and to call upon her; and he learns that she is an orphan under the guardianship of her aunt, Signora Bianchi. A few nights later he visits Ellena's home, though his only reward is to hear her sing once more and pronounce his name from the balcony. Returning home, he passes under a ruined archway where a ghostly figure clad as a monk glides across his path and warns him to stay away from the Villa Altieri, Ellena's home. Ignoring the warning, Vivaldi continues his visits, in spite of the fact that his father, the Marchese, is somehow aware of them and seconds the monk's warning. Family pride likewise inspires the Marchesa, Vivaldi's mother, to conspire with her confessor, the monk Schedoni, concerning the means by which Ellena may be separated from Vivaldi; for both mother and father are convinced that a marriage with a poor girl would taint their reputation. Vivaldi, however, gains Signora Bianchi's consent to marry the girl whose heart he had previously won.

Signora Bianchi dies under mysterious circumstances in fulfillment of another dire admonition from the archway monk which concluded with the statement that death awaited Vivaldi at Altieri. Vivaldi later nearly accuses Schedoni of being the archway monk and of having insinuated himself into Vivaldi's family to destroy its peace; but Schedoni has no trouble defending himself against Vivaldi's unsupported assertions. However, another prophecy of the archway monk is fulfilled when Vivaldi discovers that Ellena has been abducted from her home: she had been taken to a nunnery, through the machinations of Schedoni and the Marchesa. There, she is chided by the Abbess for having tried to marry into an aristocratic family; and she is told that she must either take the veil or marry a man of the Marchesa's choosing. Vivaldi seeks out Schedoni, interrupts him in the midst of his meditations, and very nearly assaults him because he supposes Schedoni had been guilty of Ellena's abduction. Vivaldi and Ellena each meet with a minor experience which turns out to have major consequences. While searching for the archway monk in the ruined fortress adjacent to the arch, Vivaldi is told (by his servant Paulo) the story of a muffled penitent whose confession had caused the confessor much anguish. The penitent will turn out to be Schedoni, and the confessor is the man who helps expose him for his crimes. Ellena finds solace in the company of a nun who turns out to be her mother.

Eventually, Vivaldi finds and rescues Ellena. However, as they are about to marry, a band of men break into the church and carry her to a lonely house on the Adriatic and him to the Inquisition chambers at Rome. Their separation is the result of a plot between Schedoni and the Marchesa which was to be consummated with the murder of Ellena. Schedoni at first tries to get Spalatro, the villainous owner of the house in which Ellena is imprisoned, to kill the girl. When Spalatro refuses, Schedoni decides to kill her in her sleeps. When he is ready to murder the sleeping girl, he discovers a miniature around her neck which contains his picture. When he awakens her, he finds out that the miniature represents her father; and he is much shaken to discover he had nearly murdered his daughter. He thereupon tries to gain the Marchesa's consent to the marriage he had previously tried to prevent, but he does not tell her that Ellena is his daughter.

Vivaldi is several times questioned by the Inquisition about his relations with Ellena and Schedoni. Eventually, with much revelation and the proliferation of characters typical of a Radcliffean dénouement, all the truth comes out, the villain dies, and the hero and heroine wed. Schedoni had been a younger son who had had his brother assassinated in order to gain his property and his wife. After he had carried her off, the wife had to marry him in order to save her honor; but when he had returned one day to find her talking with another man, he had killed her. The confession recounted by Paulo earlier had been Schedoni's confession to a confessor who had himself been the man with Schedoni's wife when Schedoni had killed her. This confessor and the archway monk (who turned against Schedoni at last) establish the main case against Schedoni. Schedoni poisons himself, and the nun Olivia reveals not only that she is the mother of Ellena but that Schedoni is *not* the father. Her first husband was Ellena's father; the false report of her death had been made in order to prevent Schedoni's taking further vengeance on her. Meanwhile, the Marchesa has died, the Marchese is reconciled to his son's marriage to Ellena, and everyone is prepared to live happily ever after.

II   *The Villain and the Villainess*

Schedoni synthesizes two sets of villains which Mrs. Radcliffe had previously kept apart to serve as foils for each other. In one synthesis, he combines parental (secular) authority with religious (spiritual) authority; in the other, he represents not only the cruel unyielding villain of the Montoni stripe but also (after he supposes that Ellena is his daughter) the vacillating middling villain (like La Motte) whose evil or self-interested ends are compromised by sporadic influxes of a naturally good human nature that Mrs. Radcliffe seemed to believe the worst of men to possess. But Schedoni's towering malignancy through the first part of the book serves as a built-in foil to the rather remotely conceived parental impulses he feels toward Ellena after he discovers their relationship. As both a secular and spiritual authority, he combines the worst of both worlds in his potential dominance over Ellena; but this potential is never really fulfilled: it is simply there to titillate the reader with a double sense of the toils Schedoni could throw about the heroine should they become necessary or should he be put into a position to use them. And, finally, the Catholic church itself, in its inquisitorial capacity, exercises absolute authority over all the participants in the novel. The real effect of Mrs. Radcliffe's double synthesis is to involve the villain in conflicting passions and loyalties which he cannot resolve because the fundamental evil which motivates his actions is now and then attenuated by good impulses.

The major criticism of Schedoni is that his character disintegrates after he is shocked into believing that he had just about killed his own daughter. The criticism is perhaps just, but what it criticizes is also justifiable, for all of Mrs. Radcliffe's villains are eventually shattered men. They do not disintegrate over so extended a period of time and space as is allotted to Schedoni, but, at the last moment, their remorse signalizes their humanity in time for them to suffer thoroughly (so we are told at any rate) the consequences of their perversion of that humanity through their lives. We are allowed to relish at length Schedoni's remorse and correlative torments which, while they considerably weaken his esthetic stature as villain simon-pure, clearly strengthen his dramatic potential as a credible human being. The mixed character he thus represents was better realized by Victor Hugo and Giuseppe Verdi in the Rigoletto figure—the morally repulsive individual whose redemption in the eyes of the reader (insofar as it can be permitted at all) is based in his love for his child.

In her previous novels Mrs. Radcliffe had described temporal evil blown up to supernatural proportions by a secular villain whose ends are predictably secular. In Schedoni, she creates a spiritual villain, in the manner of Matthew Lewis's Ambrosio in *The Monk*, who works toward secular ends through means which share in the supernatural aura with which Mrs. Radcliffe imbues the Catholic church and its representatives. He is, like Shakespeare's Iago (who is his true literary archetype), not what he is. Like all Radcliffean villains, he retains his inscrutability in spite of the relatively large amount of description applied to him. The reason for his being able to do that is that the description is in such negative terms that it adds to the obscurity which it seems to disperse: his family is unknown; he wishes "to throw an impenetrable veil over his origin. . . . He was never heard to mention a relative, or the place of his nativity, and he had artfully eluded every enquiry that approached the subject. . . ." Yet there are certain undefined circumstances which indicate that he is a man of good birth and broken fortunes: his spirit seemed lofty—Radcliffean villains are always proud, disdainfully so—when " it had sometimes looked forth from under the disguise of his manners." But this spirit "showed not . . . the aspirings of a generous mind, but rather the gloomy pride of a disappointed one." (We later discover that he had indeed been frustrated in his hopes for advancement in his vocation.) His close associates know nothing of him and must merely conjecture about the cause of his "severe reserve and unconquerable silence, his solitary habits and frequent penances," which they ascribe either to his misfortunes or to "some hideous crime gnawing upon an awakened conscience."

Schedoni is the perfect complement to the Marchesa, who is quite as prideful and quite as malignant. In the dialogues between these two, Mrs. Radcliffe best defines the character of each in a set of dramatic exchanges which in themselves and in the commentary surrounding them constitute her most subtle psychological probings into the nature of evil. The powerful and, in its way, natural union of these two proud and malignant souls delineates a kind of spiritual adultery far more profound than the actual lasciviousness ascribed to the Marchioness Mazzini in *The Sicilian Romance*. The aim of Schedoni's casuistry in these dialogues is to elicit from the Marchesa the death sentence he would like imposed on Ellena so that he could thereby gain revenge for the affront which Vivaldi had accorded him; but he himself does not want to say the words that would make him the initiator of the crime. He tells the Marchesa that Ellena and Vivaldi have wed, and she is distraught at the degradation which such an alliance imposes on her house. He seems to palliate for Vivaldi's conduct in the process of indicating its bad consequences from the Marchesa's perspective. She laments that there is no way to throw off the disgrace, and he begins to weave the web which finally implicates the Marchesa in the crime he contemplates:

"Perhaps that is affirming too much," observed Schedoni.
"How, father!" said the Marchesa.
"Perhaps a possibility does remain," said he.
"Point it out to me, good father! I do not perceive it."
"Nay, my lady," replied the subtle Schedoni, correcting himself, "I am by no means assured that such possibility does exist."
"It was cruel of you, father, to suggest a hope which you could not justify. . . . (606)

He then says that only his solicitude for her family's reputation has caused him to ferret out "some desperate means of delivering it from disgrace." The Marchesa echoes the word; is further distraught at its truth; and, when Schedoni backtracks to suggest that there is no remedy, exclaims that there should be a law to prevent such "criminal marriages." The introduction of the legal angle and the concept of justice inverts the morality of the contemplated murder in the characteristic manner of the villain. When the Marchesa says that a woman who so disgraces a family deserves a punishment nearly equal to that of a state criminal, Schedoni fills in the word she would say when he states that such a woman deserves death. They then agree that it is astonishing that the lawmakers had not provided such a penalty to protect their own honors.

The argument continues with a specious appeal to nature framed in abstract terms of justice, duty, virtue, prejudice, the general end of which is to establish the morality of the murder they are both prompted to by differing aspects of self-interest:

"Justice does not the less exist, because her laws are neglected," observed Schedoni. "A sense of what she commands lives in our breasts; and when we fail to obey that sense, it is to weakness, not to virtue, that we yield."
"Certainly," replied the Marchesa, "that truth never yet was doubted."

"Pardon me, I am not so certain as to that," said the Confessor, "when justice happens to oppose prejudice, we are apt to believe it virtuous to disobey her. For instance, though the law of justice demands the death of this girl, yet because the law of the land forbears to enforce it, you, my daughter, even you! though possessed of a man's spirit, and his clear perceptions, would think that virtue bade her live, when it was only fear!" (606)

The Marchesa then pronounces her manliness à la Lady Macbeth, intimating that she is quite ready to hear the strategy which she supposes Schedoni is on the brink of proposing, but he does not propose it. He withdraws, instead, behind the façade of a dutiful but overzealous concern with the Marchesa's house which, he says, perhaps misled his judgment and made him unjust. The reader is kept in suspense as this shuffling goes on; and, lest he mistake Schedoni's purpose in toying so with the Marchesa's distracted state of mind, Mrs. Radcliffe sets it down for him:

The Marchesa wished him to lead her back to the point from which she herself had deviated, and he seemed determined that she should lead him thither. She mused and hesitated. Her mind was not yet familiar with atrocious guilt; and the crime which Schedoni had suggested somewhat alarmed her. She feared to think and still more to name it; yet, so acutely susceptible was her pride, so stern her indignation, and so profound her desire of vengeance, that her mind was tossed as on a tempestuous ocean, and these terrible feelings threatened to overwhelm all the residue of humanity in her heart. Schedoni observed all its progressive movements, and, like a gaunt tiger, lurked in silence, ready to spring forward at the moment of opportunity. (607)

The Marchesa is forced into halting half-statements which she would like Schedoni to fill in with the direful words that he had spoken only to withdraw. "He chose," says Mrs. Radcliffe with a subtler brand of irony than she usually has at her disposal, "to spare his own delicacy rather than that of the Marchesa." The shuffling continues through several exchanges in which both the Marchesa and Schedoni skillfully avoid the statement that they and the audience are primed for. The effect of the dialogue is not only to characterize the moral duplicity of the participants but also to keep the reader in suspense, just as much as the interrupted narrative does elsewhere.

The plot's progress is delayed until the next chapter, which contains the best example in Ann Radcliffe's work of subtle psychological probing into the criminal mind. When Schedoni and the Marchesa meet in a cloister the evening after the previous indecisive dialogue, she begins with a pious exclamation lamenting the misery her son had brought on his family. In her misfortune she turns, as she says, to her "only disinterested friend"—the adjective represents the ultimate ironic inversion of ethical standards in the Radcliffean novel. Schedoni directs an aside at the Marchesa's husband which allows the latter to be rationalized out of their scheme on the ground of his "prejudices." The devil can make apt use of the sentimental scripture and shibboleths. Mrs. Radcliffe often laments the prejudice of those—like nuns and abbots—who work against nature and a true perception of God's will—and so the Marchesa characterizes her husband. He is victimized by a conventional moral education which keeps him from deviating from its principles even when circumstances demand a revision of stereotyped moral incentives to action. He would not, that is, recognize that the ends justify the means.

The tone of the dialogue is set by the church background, by the relationship between the two (confessor-confessee), by the continual special pleading for a moral sanction to their act which they hope their own consciences will grant them in consequence of their mutually tendentious arguments. Schedoni points out that, if Ellena had been condemned by law, the justice of their action could not be more certain. The Marchesa notes that, in fact, the law does not sanction their contemplated murder; "and the boldest virtue may pause, when it reaches the utmost verge of safety." Schedoni—who is referred to as "the Confessor" through most of the dialogue—answers the Marchesa's reservation with a triumphant avowal of virtue's omnipotence that could serve differing purposes in *Paradise Lost*, *Comus*, or the *Areopagitica*: "Never! . . . virtue never trembles; it is her glory, and sublimest attribute to be superior to danger; to despise it. The best principle is not virtue till it reaches this elevation" (608). We remember the rather shady claim to dialectical prowess his fellow monks accorded Schedoni, for he is particularly adept at making the worse appear the better cause. Unlike the generalized and unsubstantiated attributes piled indiscriminately into the account of most Radcliffean villains, Schedoni's claims to infamy are illustrated in practice. But Mrs. Radcliffe is not content with letting Schedoni's warmth and the Marchesa's moral calculus stand as mere sophistry or hypocrisy; she has a deeper psychological insight in view; and, though she remains primly enigmatic in suggesting it, she makes it fairly clear what we should make of this exchange by telling us what a surface reading of it would be: "A philosopher might, perhaps, have been surprised to hear two persons seriously defining the limits of virtue, at the very moment in which they meditated the most atrocious crime; a man of the world would have considered it to be mere hypocrisy; a supposition which might have disclosed his general knowledge of manners, but would certainly have betrayed his ignorance of the human heart" (608).

Even villains have human hearts; and, because they have them, they eventually pay for their crimes before they die. Schedoni and the Marchesa have already indicated a certain esthetic or moral distaste for the word "murder" which appropriately labels their designs. Elsewhere each finds it comforting to believe in the virtue of the other because such a belief helps each to think better of himself. When Schedoni finally discovers a genuine human affection in himself, he may lose his supernatural coloring, but he restores the reader's confidence in essential human nature. The moral *expliqué* requires that inhuman actions or motivations turn out to be not the result of supernatural infernal forces but of a human heart which had been perverted by wrong thinking. When the heart rights itself, the villain is in one way or another destroyed.

Because of the Marchesa's superstitious reactions to churchly accoutrements and manifestations—a confessional inscription reading "God hears thee" and a requiem for the dead—Schedoni leaves this tryst incensed at women's inconstancy of purpose. The decision is delayed, the suspense maintained; but the end is already dreadfully apparent to the reader's anticipations. As it is to the reader—and to other characters, good and evil—"suspense is to [the Marchesa] the purgatory of this world. . . ."

Schedoni's contempt for the Marchesa's vacillation is paid off later when, like her, he proves sufficiently a "slave to the passions" to let his heart interfere with his plan to murder Ellena. In the dialogue which follows his failure, the Marchesa is remarkably adept at gauging the deception implicit in Schedoni's ambiguous attempts to avoid admitting he had not done the deed without

[143]

actually lying. Mrs. Radcliffe again obtrudes her moral insistence that evil natures must feel remorse for their evil thoughts and deeds by providing Schedoni with a shudder as he enters the presence of the would-be murderer of his daughter, and the Marchesa averts her gaze from him because she believes that *he* is very likely a murderer. Schedoni, we are told, had been for once taught to think justly; but such thinking does not extend to his exchanges with the Marchesa, which finally lead him from ambiguity into positive lying about the place at which he has deposited Ellena.

Mrs. Radcliffe works several psychological effects and inferences into their conversation. Schedoni clearly finds himself in an uncomfortable position because he must now controvert his previous argument concerning the justice of killing Ellena. Because there is a natural correspondence between evil minds—as Mrs. Radcliffe states in *The Romance of the Forest*—the Marchesa intuitively perceives the shuffling of which Schedoni is now guilty. On the other hand, because she recognizes that, for such natures as hers and Schedoni's, self-interest is the mainspring of all action, she cannot understand why he has apparently worked against his own interest by betraying hers. The overall moral inference is that, once a tincture of good nature stains the fabric of a moral universe that is woven out of self-interested motives, such a universe begins to fall apart along with the characters of those who make it up.

The dramatic interest of the dialogue revolves around the notion of an evil character, Schedoni, who is attempting to groom his newly found parental affections so that they accord with his self-interested ends. The conversation between the two is intermitted by omniscient probings into the minds of both which serve to heighten the general tenor of the suspense aroused by the question which the novel consistently poses: how will all this affect Ellena? The Marchesa's acuteness in detecting Schedoni's flawed immorality may frustrate our hopes for Ellena, as it does his; but its strictly Gothic purpose is to titillate the reader much as similar debates over the fate of the heroine do in other novels. That is, as in *The Sicilian Romance, The Romance of the Forest*, and *Udolpho*, the victimized heroine must depend on an essentially evil agency for some relative good. The difference between the situation here and in previous novels is that the conflict between self-interested powers over the heroine is compounded because Schedoni's motives are confused; his power is made weaker by the disinterest which paradoxically tinctures them. The Marchesa's immediate superiority rests on the consistency of her self-interested motives, which have apparently overcome the parental affections that have humanized Schedoni with an inner conflict he cannot resolve.

III   *The Villain and the Hero*

Schedoni's dialogues with the Marchesa portray the before and after of a dominant evil nature infiltrated by an unsuspected goodness which is finally bent to serve self-interested purposes. His dialogue with Vivaldi dramatizes both his adroitness at handling an impetuous and ingenuous youth and his inability to understand the motives behind the ingenuousness he makes use of. The end result of the dialogue is to establish Schedoni's Machiavellian bad nature and Vivaldi's overly sanguine good nature. But Mrs. Radcliffe is, meanwhile, as much concerned with emphasizing the relatively good qualities which the monk presents as she is in letting the expansive and good nature of her hero eventually shine through the tactless gaucheries that his rash and uninformed questioning of Schedoni lead him into. A secondary but more immediate result of the dialogue is additional confusion of the reader concerning the relationship between (or identity of) the archway monk and Schedoni.

Mrs. Radcliffe gives us and Vivaldi reason both to doubt and to affirm that Schedoni is the archway monk. While the empirical evidence seems to weigh against the suspicion, the obscurity in which the monk had been involved whenever he had appeared to Vivaldi allows an inkling of a doubt to remain lurking in the reader's mind. He can entertain the possibility that he may later be surprised into discountenancing contrary inferences drawn from enshrouded fact by a clear assurance that Schedoni *is* the man his diabolical demeanor fits him to be. The implicit doubt that Mrs. Radcliffe hopes she is instilling in her reader's mind is confirmed by her previous characterization of Schedoni as a man for whom empirical reality and logical inference were matter and method which he distorted and transcended to suit his malignant ends. The fact that Vivaldi is sufficiently objective in his evaluation of the evidence regarding the possible identity of the two monks leads us at first to accept the intuitive leap he makes into direct accusation of Schedoni as his secret enemy. In retrospect, the reader sees that the leap he took was not at all grounded in the reasons he had adduced. And the rashness which Schedoni then takes advantage of had really led Vivaldi into the accusation which his own good nature soon leads him to renounce and condemn.

The passage is worth quoting at length because it is typical of those in which Mrs. Radcliffe gives her hero (or heroine) the rational inferences he needs to discriminate truth from fancy—and her reader the sense that alternatives have been exhausted before a particularly terrible or ominous conclusion has been arrived at:

[Vivaldi's] eye and his ear assisted him to conjecture at least, if not to obtain the information he wished; and, as he listened to the deep tones of Schedoni's voice, he became almost certain that they were not the accents of his unknown adviser, though he considered at the same moment that it was not difficult to disguise or to feign a voice. His stature seemed to decide the question more reasonably; for the figure of Schedoni appeared taller than that of the stranger; and though there was something of resemblance in their air, which Vivaldi had never observed before, he again considered, that the habit of the same order, which each wore, might easily occasion an artificial resemblance. Of the likeness, as to countenance, he could not judge, since the stranger's had been so much shrouded by his cowl that Vivaldi had never distinctly seen a single feature. Schedoni's hood was now thrown back, so that he could not compare even the air of their heads under similar circumstances; but as he remembered to have seen the confessor on a former day approaching his mother's closet with the cowl shading his face, the same gloomy severity was drawn on his fancy. Yet this again might be only an artificial effect, a character which the cowl alone gave to the head; and any face seen imperfectly beneath its dark shade might have appeared equally severe. Vivaldi was still extremely perplexed in his opinion. One circumstance, however, seemed to throw some light on his judgment. The stranger had appeared in the habit of a monk, and, if Vivaldi's transient observation might be trusted, he was of the very same order with that of Schedoni. Yet if he were Schedoni, or even his agent, it was not probable that he would have shown himself in a dress that might lead to a discovery of his person. That he was anxious for concealment his manner strongly proved; it seemed then that this habit of a monk was only a disguise assumed for the purpose of misleading conjecture. (552–53)

"Misleading conjecture" is Mrs. Radcliffe's forte and her purpose here. A variant form of it appears elsewhere in the compilations of dire alternatives—most of which would only occur to the fancy or sensibility of a Radcliffean heroine. The single effect of both forms is to keep the truth in obscurity and the reader in suspense.

Vivaldi's perplexity about the monk and Schedoni confirms the reader in his own. A ray of light is admitted only to be soon lost in the obscurity it had for a moment threatened to clarify. The Burkean esthetic is clearly at work: the longer we are kept in obscurity, the longer we are kept suspended between the horrible and the sublime. Mrs. Radcliffe grooms Burke to fit her literary and psychological purpose by letting her characters reason their way through the surface mist of obscurity only to plunge themselves farther into the darker reaches of a more profound mystery which the feeble light of reason—like the feeble candles in winding Gothic corridors—illuminates only enough to heighten its possible terrors.

Correspondingly, Mrs. Radcliffe uses the reflective powers of her chief characters for the purpose of arousing in the reader a sense of the possibilities of a given situation, with reservations closing in on and hedging each clarification. Conjecture balances and opposes conjecture, rather than their developing and assisting each other toward any assured conclusion. The goal ideally attained is a dead end where inner dialectic exits into the mystery it was trying to resolve. But much has been gained: the reader has been put into full possession of alternatives, the evidence pointing each and every way—and the confusion and doubts are as exciting and suspenseful as before. They now have the added dimension provided by the fact that every rational attempt has been made to dissipate them without success.

Mrs. Radcliffe's handling of the first set of Gothic incidents, the recurrent appearance of the monk at the archway, full of warnings and prescience, are awkward strainings in the direction of the full-blown Gothic effects she arrives at with Schedoni, Spalatro, and the Inquisition. They may titillate at first, but they become tedious after a while, particularly when the initial association with the Ghost scene in *Hamlet* fails to add to the effect because of the near-plagiarism that the verbal and scenic parallels suggest to the reader. The cowl-shrouded monk names Vivaldi, warns him, disappears; and, along with some suggestion that the figure they have seen is like air, invulnerable, Vivaldi and his partner convert to Hamlet and Horatio on the ramparts: "Let us follow!" cried Vivaldi; and he began to ascend. "Stop, for Heaven's sake, stop!" said Bonarmo (544). Later, when Vivaldi returns, shaken, Bonarmo-Horatio asks what he has seen to be so affected; and Vivaldi-Hamlet tells him to ask him no questions. Mrs. Radcliffe apparently relied on her readers' using their Shakespeare associations to heighten her horrors; but, like her Claudean and Salvatorean landscapes, her Shakespearean echoes lose their effectiveness because of their insistent omnipresence. For all their ghostly apparitions, bloodstains, ominous warnings, and sheer obscurity, the archway scenes are in themselves examples of the kind of contrived and superficial terrorism which Mrs. Radcliffe generally left to her imitators. She was capable of more subtle effects.

The next appearance of the monk merges with the excessive sensibility theme to expand the esthetic and moral value of Mrs. Radcliffe's sensationalism. The monk pops out of the gloom on cue as Vivaldi passes the arch and warns him not to go to Altieri because there is death in the house. While the ailing Bianchi is clearly the body most likely to be dead, Vivaldi tortures himself with a vision of Emily's corpse: "He saw her wounded and bleeding to death; saw her ashy countenance and her wasting eyes, from which the spirit of life was fast departing, turned piteously on himself as if imploring him to save her from the fate that was dragging her to the grave" (549). So vivid is this mistaken vision that, when he gets to the house, he can barely summon the resolution to enter. When Vivaldi finally staggers into the house, he is met by the servant who plays an ambiguous "she" reference for all its worth to Vivaldi—and maybe for much more than it can be worth to the modern reader, whether indifferent or sympathetic. But ambiguity, which is close kin to obscurity, is another device categorized under suspense in the Radcliffean repertoire.

Almost swooning, Vivaldi drags himself, as in a Kafkian nightmare, to the room in which he finds Ellena mourning for the dead Bianchi. Even now Vivaldi cannot relieve himself of his tension by expressing his ecstasy, but Mrs. Radcliffe lets us know it is there through a macabre paradox—"the same event which excited her grief accidently inspired his joy." Such variations on the contrarious passions displayed in heroes and heroines at climactic (or even anticlimactic) moments are the psychological counterparts to Mrs. Radcliffe's Claudean-Salvatorean landscapes, where beauty smiles in the lap of terror because both are most effective in contrasted combination. Adroitly handled, contrast is the fundamental rhetorical means through which Mrs. Radcliffe expresses her many-faceted art. It is the basic pattern of her sentiment, her surprise, and her suspense.

IV   *The Heroine: Beauty in the Lap of Terror*

When Ellena is borne away to a convent by three men, masked and ominously silent, she moves through landscape essentially sublime—because it is meant to condition the terror which she feels—but it is environed here and there with beauty. The purpose of the contrast in nature is to parallel the psychological progression from relative tranquility to the turmoil which villains and their obscure agents inspire in their victims. Throughout an extensive descriptive passage, the reader is kept in touch with Ellena's esthetic and moral responses to what she sees:

It was when the heat and the light were declining that the carriage entered a rocky defile which showed, as through a telescope reversed, distant plains and mountains opening beyond, lighted up with all the purple splendour of the sun. Along this deep and shadowy perspective, a river, which was seen descending among the cliffs of a mountain, rolled with impetuous force, fretting and foaming amidst the dark rocks in its descent and then flowing in a limpid lapse to the brink of other precipices, whence again it fell with thundering strength to the abyss, throwing its misty clouds of spray high in the air and seeming to claim the sole empire of this solitary wild. Its bed took up the whole breadth of the chasm, which some strong convulsion of the earth seemed to have formed, not leaving space even for a road along its margin. The road, therefore, was carried high among the cliffs that impended over the river and seemed as if suspended in air; while the gloom and vastness of the precipices, which towered above and sunk below it, together with the amazing force and uproar of the falling waters, combined to render the pass more terrific than the pencil could describe or language can express. Ellena ascended it, not with indifference but with calmness; she experienced somewhat of a dreadful pleasure in looking down upon the irresistible flood; but this emotion was heightened into awe when she perceived that the road led to a slight bridge which, thrown across the chasm at an immense height, united two opposite cliffs, between which the whole cataract of the river descended. The bridge, which was defended only by a slender railing, appeared as if hung amidst the clouds. Ellena, while she was crossing it, almost forgot her misfortunes. Having reached the opposite side of the glen, the road gradually descended the precipices for about half a mile, when it opened to extensive prospects over plains and towards distant mountains—the sunshine landscape, which had long appeared to bound the shadowy pass. The transition was as the passage through the vale of death to the bliss of eternity; but the idea of its resemblance did not long remain with Ellena. Perched high among the cliffs of a mountain, which might be said to terminate one of the jaws of this terrific gorge, and which was one of the loftiest of a chain that surrounded the plains, appeared the spires and long terraces of a monastery; and she soon understood that her journey was to conclude there. (559)

Mrs. Radcliffe is making her picture move through the perspective and emotions of her heroine by combining esthetic reaction with ethical commentary. The succession of pictures through which the coach passes comprise a picture gallery in which the spectator becomes both participant in and interpreter of the variously pleasing or awe-inspiring vistas that open to her either at once or in succession. Words and phrases like "showed," "a telescope reversed," "the purple splendour of the setting sun," "the deep and shadowy perspective," and "the sunshine landscape" define the pictorial view of her subject that Mrs. Radcliffe takes, while Ellena's calmness, her "dreadful pleasure," her self-forgetfulness hint at the moral qualities of the esthetic object. The esthetic and moral are merged in a contrast that also indicates that all we have been given has come to us from Ellena who idealizes the composite travelogue as "the passage through the vale of death to the bliss of eternity."

Contrasting pictures of nature and human environment are succeeded by contrasting reasons to fear and delight at once in a given circumstance or action when Ellena arrives at her destination. The general sense of gloom, oppressive authority, perverted instincts, and tendentious reasoning which permeate the monastery center on the figure of the abbess. She finds her foil in the "favorite nun," Ellena's mother, as does the monastery itself in the contrasted "serene and majestic" nature which Ellena can view from her favorite turret, which, like the room in other novels, is the place where she can retreat for an antidote from the miseries of the social world. Solacing herself in her turret one day, Ellena is at least as surprised as we are when a strain of music in the air turns out to emanate from none other than Vivaldi, who is perched on a precipice, strumming his guitar. Again, lest we be betrayed into unqualified joy at his appearance, we are told that Ellena cannot but be alarmed at his "tremendous situation."

The scene is no sooner set for escape and consequent happiness than Olivia, the good nun, tells Ellena that the abbess had decided to imprison Ellena in a dungeon cell from which no one had ever returned. Once introduced, the unpleasing prospect recurs for various purposes. At the moment, it serves a sentimental moral purpose by offering Olivia a chance to recall her kindness to a nun who had languished in this cell for two years; Olivia, against orders, had spoken to that nun. Ellena praises her noble action, but Olivia sententiously observes—possibly illustrating the bad effects of her scholastic environment, possibly illustrating her thoroughgoing humility in the face of praise—that she did it partly out of self-interest, her motive for warning Ellena; for she could not bear the agony of pity, which not only runneth soon in gentil heart, but is "also keener than any other, except for that of remorse." Remorse, we recall, is the villain's comeuppance. Later, during the escape, Ellena passes what she supposes to be this very cell, so that it serves not only to elicit sympathetic pity from the reader but also sympathetic terror. The economy of means to opposed ends is typical of Mrs. Radcliffe, for she seldom allows an event, possible or actual, to occur or not occur without its emotive potential being fully used. Where the event does not occur, the imaginative potential implicit in any reference to it is far greater than it is for events which merely take place and thereby exhaust, in part, their usefulness.

The escape itself is engineered with as fastidious an eye for the adventitious and the horrifying possibility as Mrs. Radcliffe ever turned toward a single incident. It is in the tradition of the near-nightmare movements from dungeon cell to open air that Mrs. Radcliffe initiated in *The Castles of Athlin and Dunbayne*. The plan is for Vivaldi to pass a message through a grate to Ellena which will tell her where to meet him, but everything goes as wrong as it can without actually frustrating the escape. The grate is in a parlor full of nuns; and, in order to make herself known to Vivaldi from among the others, Ellena reveals herself—but to the wrong man. However, she is not betrayed. Vivaldi finally appears; the note is placed inside the grate; but, before Ellena can pick it up, a passing nun wafts it to the ground where Ellena must leave it until the group breaks up.

The usual horrors run through her mind in the interim: the plot is found out, Vivaldi is seized, this monk knows, that nun knows, the abbess knows. But no one knows, nor does anyone get to know what the message says even after Ellena retrieves it and carries it to her chamber. In the midst of her trembling eagerness to open and read the all-important note, her sole candle goes out; and, like Adeline in *The Romance of the Forest*, she dare not ask for another light. In the Radcliffean world, the little things in life are as frustrating as the big ones are terrifying. Mrs. Radcliffe again succinctly sums up the crucial irony of Ellena's predicament: "she experienced all the various tortures that the consciousness of having in her very hand the information on a timely knowledge of which her life, perhaps, depended, without being able to understand it, could inflict" (590). The reader suffers too, but not for long, since Olivia soon comes, with the requisite candle.

One crux solved establishes the condition for another. Time is essential; much of it has been wasted; and will Vivaldi still be waiting? Ellena and Olivia pass through the heart of enemy country, the passages and halls and stairways of the convent, even to a confrontation with the abbess. But, beyond hope (and credence), all goes well enough to bring Ellena on time to the trysting place, though at every step she is sure that her strength will never carry her another—and, at sight of the very doorway beyond which Vivaldi should be, she is doubly sure that she cannot make the last few yards. The joy she feels on hearing Vivaldi's voice serves mainly to contrast the succeeding nightmare progress through another set of gloomy and secret corridors, which are abetted in their deviousness by an ambiguous guide who gives every indication of leading them on only to betray them. Assorted added attractions—a series of cantankerous locks and the previously mentioned cell of the languishing nun are the highlights— help exact all of the essential terror out of the situation (as heightened both by natural suspense and Ellena's morbid associative patterns). A kind of *deus ex machina* appears on the scene to lead them from gloom and miserable expectation to the moonlight world without, where "the tranquillity of the landscape below afforded an affecting contrast with the tumult and alarm of their minds."

A brief respite from terror does not mean a respite from trial for the heroine. She has survived icy fear; but how will she cope with fiery desire? Vivaldi wants to marry her on the spot, but conditions are not auspicious, however expedient they may seem. Vivaldi has just managed her escape against odds; he loves her; she loves him; he deserves her esteem and respect; only evil agencies militate against their union. Yet she must say no—at least, at first—and when she does, with many doubts and grim forebodings, yield to expedience, her previous hesitancy is justified when at the very altar she is caught up and carried off to Spalatro's cottage. Of course, the positive aspect of this sudden plunge from the prospect of tainted bliss into dire calamity is that Ellena will be saved for a marriage which will be absolutely ideal. Even the Marchese will consent to it. Before then, however, both she and Vivaldi must suffer through their worst trials apart from each other.

After a short pastoral interlude (apt contrast preparatory to a plunge into horror), Ellena comes close enough to Spalatro's cottage to be told that she "will soon be at the end of . . . [her] journey and at rest." There was a time when Mrs. Radcliffe would have called attention to these ominous ambiguities, but she now leaves them alone to work their effect on her readers' much-conditioned associations. Silence, solitude, and decay characterize the "ancient and peculiar structure." Spalatro answers the door with a visage "so misery-struck that Ellena could not look upon it with indifference, though wrapt in misery of her own." This is a heightened dimension of the usual capacity of the heroine to forget her troubles in those of another, for Spalatro has no claim on her affections; indeed, his appearance promises her the kind of treatment she has learned to expect from the mysterious agencies that move her about from place to place without her consent: "The lamp he held threw a gleam athwart [his face] and showed the gaunt ferocity of famine, to which the shadow of his hollow eyes added a terrific wildness. Ellena shrunk while she gazed. She had never before seen villainy and suffering so strongly pictured on the same face, and she observed him with a degree of thrilling curiosity which for a moment excluded from her mind all consciousness of the evils to be apprehended from him" (625). After a fainting fit, induced by her inferences that they will kill her there, she is brought to a room with a mattress (like that, we recall, which was in the cell of the languishing nun), cobwebs (unswept for many years), a single grated window—"Such preparation for preventing escape seemed to hint how much there might be to escape from."

The murder attempt itself is conditioned first by the afflicted conscience of Spalatro, who has somehow and to some small extent been affected by the virtue of Ellena. He is much censured by Schedoni, who, however, is himself much shaken, as Mrs. Radcliffe indicates by repeated examples of his forgetfulness and his obvious fears. Entering into Ellena's room, Schedoni suffers the same kind of fears which heroes and heroines suffer when in the presence of evil or its agencies. He sees her innocent countenance, she smiles, he draws back—"She smiles in her murderer's face"— and he shudders. She cries, she speaks, he again draws back. Mrs. Radcliffe's point is twofold: the villain cannot escape his humanity; all this humanity is perverted by the evil occasion for its manifestation.

And she also makes it clear that all the strength of character which one would ascribe to Schedoni is perverted to the evil act which concludes for him in frustration and horror, much like the feelings usually allowed to heroines alone: "His agitation and repugnance to strike increased with every moment of delay, and, as often as he prepared to plunge the poignard in her bosom a shuddering horror restrained him. Astonished at his own feelings and indignant at what he termed a dastardly weakness, he found it necessary to argue with himself, and his rapid thoughts said, 'Do I not feel the necessity of this act! Does not what is dearer to me than existence—does not my consequence depend on the execution of it?' " (636).

Mrs. Radcliffe's point is clear, though perhaps not well made through the inner dialectic of a man she has developed as a subtle reasoner. He is motivated by all bad passions—pride and self-interest, most of all—to perform this act. His moments of truth and horror occur at once: "after gazing an instant, some new cause of horror seemed to seize all his frame, and he stood for some moments aghast and motionless like a statue. His respiration was short and laborious, chilly drops stood on his forehead, and all his faculties of mind seemed suspended. When he recovered, he stopped to examine again the miniature, which had occasioned this revolution, and which had lain concealed beneath the lawn that he withdrew" (636). This is the miniature that seemingly proves him Ellena's father. She wakes at his call, and a heavy-handed display of sentimental irony leads her to address him according to his garb as "father," though she at first takes him for her murderer as well. Schedoni gives way to tears, confesses himself her father, and for several pages he is made to suffer the consequences of the act he nearly committed. When Ellena consistently praises him as her savior, her gratitude simply aggravates his remorse. Mrs. Radcliffe draws out her villain's punishment through tedious interplays and forced ironies that overmake her point.

The murder scene and its prelude elicit the pity and terror that Mrs. Radcliffe is concerned most with portraying. They also contrast the affective virtue of Ellena, whose innocence is her shield, with the viciousness exiting into remorse which characterizes Schedoni. Since the full esthetic and full ethical ends are served, the section is a moral as well as an esthetic triumph. And both ends had to be served for it to succeed in the eyes of Mrs. Radcliffe and her critics.

V The Testing of the Hero

When Vivaldi's captors lead him into Rome at carnival time, Mrs. Radcliffe's pictorial sense of contrasting elements, as matter for irony as well as for esthetic effect, enters into both the psychological and physical setting. The gaiety outside is constrasted with Vivaldi's inner torment, which, predictably, is less the result of his own condition and its dire promise than of his "dreadful uncertainty" concerning the fate of her he loved. The gaiety is contrasted with the severe aspect of the guards, who scorned the frivolity of the scene and so heightened their inhumanity. A succeeding contrast introduces the Gothic element that expands as the group approaches the Inquisition castle. The sight of Rome's magnificent ruins, "those gigantic skeletons, which once enclosed a soul, whose energies governed a world," inspired Vivaldi with a "melancholy awe, a sacred enthusiasm, that withdrew him from himself." The effect parallels that which Ellena had experienced when she entered the terrific gorge leading to her first imprisonment.

The Inquisition castle itself is full of the sublime in the gloomy-lofty sense, walls of "immense height," "innumerable massy bulwarks," no windows, no grates, "but a vast and dreary blank," with only a single "small round tower breaking their monotony." The inscrutable blind face of the obscure, gigantic structure is the outward symbol of the minds at work inside it. Adding to the suggestive malignancy of its foreboding aspect is the porter, a "grim-visaged, comfortless despair," who appropriately stands guardian over a portal eventually leading to the chamber which Vivaldi envisages as inscribed "Abandon all hope, ye who enter here." The usual paraphernalia of the Gothic interior is implemented by the accoutrements of mystery and torment which suggest the specific trials which Vivaldi may soon face.

The emphasis is on death and the possibility of it. There is a "deathlike silence" in the vestibule which reminded Vivaldi of what he had heard of the "burial vaults" of the Inquisition; he feels that he walks in the "chambers of the dead," which seemed never to have been "the residence of the living." Dark-clad figures, real or imaginary, seem to come and go in the gloom; Vivaldi hears a "half-stifled groan" as of someone in agony; small lamps "feebly penetrate" the gloom of the passage. Another description of the demonic visages of the inquisitors and warders he sees about him leads him to exclaim against the inhumanity man shows to man.

The occasion is hardly sufficient for the outburst, but it is enough to engage and demonstrate Vivaldi's sensibility. And that is its purpose, for he forgets his own sufferings in contemplating the sufferings of others. "A new view of human nature seemed to burst at once upon his mind"; and, instead of giving in to misanthropy, he gains a resolution which is supposed to indicate his moral growth under the trials and imaginings then afflicting him: "His passions, thus restrained, seemed to become virtues, and to display themselves in the energy of his courage and his fortitude. His soul became stern and vigorous in despair" (620). It is the thought of Emily that helps condition this positive response. Even the guards are awed by his calm dignity and the "strength of his intellectual self." However evil, inscrutable, and scornful, villains and their factotums may be, they invariably acknowledge

moral and spiritual superiority when it shows itself in their cap-
tives or victims.

Vivaldi faces the Inquisition several times and returns to a
Gothic dungeon in the interims. The inquisitorial room and its inhabitants are detailed in gloom edging into a blackness compounded when, on occasion, Vivaldi is blindfolded. The inquisitors, variations on Schedoni, are dressed in black, have piercing
eyes—one inquisitor has a black turban heightening the "natural
ferocity of his visage." Vague horrors abound in such a setting—
a gigantic crucifix is offset in its spiritual implications by "some
instruments of singular appearance," whose precise function is left
to the reader's imagination. Not only is silence the condition of
the Inquisition, but it is demanded as well from Vivaldi, who
must swear not to relate what goes on in the examination chamber.

Both the inscrutability of the inquisitors and their sporadic justice assist the detective-story finale of the novel. They not only
unravel the complicated mysteries Mrs. Radcliffe has so far spun
for us, but they also assure Schedoni a fair trial. The blind rigor
of their inquisitional techniques on the spiritual level corresponds
with the narrow-principled moral notions the Marchese illustrates
on the secular level. And, as Vivaldi is capable of loving his father
in spite of the latter's perverse ethic, so he can appreciate to the
point of tears humane justice even when filtered through religious
purblindness: "Are these the sentiments of an Inquisitor! . . . can
such glorious candour appear amidst the tribunal of an Inquisition!" (688). But, as "tears fall fast on Vivaldi's cheek," we are
reminded that it is, after all, his own disinterestedness that is the
moral virtue predominant here: "Vivaldi could not have felt more
esteem and admiration if he had been the one towards whom the
candour had been shown." Mrs. Radcliffe's concern is not to vin-
dicate the Catholic church, Schedoni, or even the Marchese. She
is, however, aware that moral honesty and esthetic subtlety require
her to avoid stereotype whenever convenient.

Vivaldi's successive trips to the inquisitional chamber are intermitted with real and imagined terrors that bear on the dénouement which they help keep in suspense. In much the same way
that Adeline's reading of the fragmented manuscript in *The Romance of the Forest* is broken off by ghostly visitation or the routine evils of the real world, previsionary dreams, bloody poignards,
enigmatic messages or warnings, and monkish visitors keep Vi-

valdi and the reader well terrified even in moments of relative calm. Mrs. Radcliffe makes use of Catholicism as if its impenetrable mysteries were as unnatural and potentially diabolical as any evil agents she could import from a merely illusory supernatural. The natural and para-supernatural terrors suffered by her heroes and heroines coalesce in one context of sublunary power which has a truly spiritual sublimity permeating the superstitious fears it inspires.

The implication is that, while human agencies, as always, are responsible for the ghostly manifestations wandering about ruined arches or inquisitional chambers, their pretensions to spiritual authority connect them with the subliminal reaches of man's psychic makeup wherein primitive fears of the supernatural are conceived and nourished. And, like these dark places of the mind, the church is delightfully obscure as well as unnatural in its operations. But the unnatural is never the supernatural, nor are any of its effects. As Schedoni dwindles into a specimen of humanity destroyed by unnatural actions and passions, the para-supernatural dwindles into the rational *expliqués* which irritated readers who failed to understand the criticism Mrs. Radcliffe obliquely leveled at them when she rather primly pronounced on Vivaldi's unwillingness to accept a world where cause and effect were providentially and naturally ordered:

His imagination, thus elevated by wonder and painful curiosity, was prepared for something above the reach of common conjecture and beyond the accomplishment of human agency. His understanding was sufficiently clear and strong to detect many errors of opinion that prevailed around him, as well as to despise the common superstitions of his country, and, in the usual state of his mind, he probably would not have paused for a moment on the subject before him; but his passions were now interested and his fancy awakened, and though he was unconscious of the propensity, he would, perhaps, have been somewhat disappointed to have descended suddenly from the region of fearful sublimity to which he had soared—the world of terrible shadows—to the earth, on which he daily walked and to an explanation simply natural. (557)

CHAPTER 8

Evaluation and Influence

I Moral Sensibility and the Supernatural

ANN RADCLIFFE both aided and restrained the explosion into Romanticism which characterized the 1790's. The unique popularity of her work was due not simply to her sporadic forays into sensationalism—to her surprises, suspenses, and terrors; it was due also to her ability to tone down these essentially Romantic exuberances by harmonizing them with the general tenor of Neo-classical principles of art and life which she accepted with only minor modification. She offered a respectable outlet for an officially repressed desire for the unnatural and the unconventional by merely intimating the supernatural and the grossly immoral while invariably vindicating nature, reason, and decorum.

A girl as sensitive to the good and bad in nature as an Emily or an Adeline is required to live through the kind of world which unnatural minds create for her. The evil human agents, like Montalt and Montoni, direct the action, set up the decor, and convert the rational into the inexplicable. When they distort the real world by foisting their irregular conceptions on it, this distortion is perceived by the heroine who is then forced to the conclusion that irrational and even supernatural powers are behind the obscure and certainly unnatural phenomena she lives through. But bad nature disintegrates finally. The natural order of things is vindicated, virtue and reason triumph, and the supernatural is explicated as the effect of an evil nature on a good but delicate sensibility.

Ann Radcliffe's world is preeminently one in which the limits of empirical morality and metaphysics have been reached. The senses are no longer a just criterion of what they see. Morally speaking, the world does indeed seem to be given over to evil powers who govern it for their own selfish ends. And it is their moral distortions impinging on a refined sensibility that cause it to ascribe validity, in spite of reason, to empirical phenomena which the senses are too disordered (or too limited) to define clearly.

The popular conception of the world as dream, which eighteenth-century empiricism (Berkeley's most of all) had appeared to formulate, justified a Gothic variation in which the world became nightmare to the appropriate sensibility under unnatural conditions. Perception was all, even when it was not enough. Even the natural world became, to perception, a congeries of unstable sense impressions. If the world of sight and common sense was therefore unstable, what could one cling to for affirmation of a natural and permanent order in things? There was the moral order, on one hand, and the esthetic world on the other. And they tended to complement each other to shore up a disintegrating sense world. Together, they affirmed a spiritual world which was not available to sight but could be suggested by it.

The argument from nature up to God was not rationally or empirically based in a typical Radcliffean set piece affirming divine Providence; it was rooted in an esthetic insight which contended for an ethical and benevolent God-power who would mysteriously bring good out of evil in spite of the malevolence and impercipience of man. The proof of His existence was, on one hand, the sublimity of nature and, on the other, the moral integrity of the heroine. And, always, the *expliqué* of the supernatural and the congruent revelation of the villain's designs empirically and rationally confirm the well-ordered world only momentarily disturbed in the mind of the percipient heroine. After living through the nightmare world of a Salvatorean landscape, she returned at last to the dreamy bliss of a Claude.

Like Wordsworth after her, Mrs. Radcliffe went to the poets to redeem from the wreck of the world the beauty in nature and the moral disinterestedness in human beings that mechanical physicists and pre-Utilitarian ethics had atomized into geometric and self-interested calculations which denied the spiritual unity of man and nature. Mrs. Radcliffe affirmed that unity, though she was quite unaware of the profound consequences of her affirmation. But she did provide a hint to later writers more resolutely idealistic and Romantic than she was of methods of fusion and development which were quite beyond her powers of conception. A firm belief in the principle of beauty in nature and man led her and them to affirm the esthetic road to ethical action which

Wordsworth outlined in "Tintern Abbey" and which Keats asserted at the end of the "Grecian Urn."

All in all, then, Mrs. Radcliffe's moral and social conservatism did not interfere with her relatively avant-garde sympathies with enthusiasm, imagination, nature, and even a few democratic principles. There were certainly contradictions, had she cared to ferret them out; but the confused transitional period she wrote through found it morally and esthetically convenient to bridge gaps rather than widen them. Her editorial resolution of the imminent dilemmas that could result from her rival allegiances to a moribund Rationalism and an embryonic Romanticism are bound to seem forced to a reader aware of their incompatibility. But they were natural enough from the short-range view she and her contemporaries were obliged to take of them. The general thesis her novels seem to affirm supposed that reason and conventional morality, when rightly conceived, confirmed *some* truths of nature apprehended by the enthusiastic imaginations of writers like Shaftesbury and Rousseau. Such pre-Romantic philosophers, often in different and sometimes opposed ways, managed to work out a heartfelt rationale for the esthetic insights to which contemporary poets like Thomson, Collins, and Gray were currently ascribing a species of moral truth.

Mrs. Radcliffe's epigraphs and occasional allusions quietly affirm her allegiance to the underground Romantic poetry of the era just passed. The body of her text illustrates her feelings that these writers were expressing fundamental truths about human nature which could generally be subsumed under conventional rationales or moral codes. But, unless these codes were now and then inspected by reference to the benevolent heart or to "nature," they lost their spiritual warrant and became arbitrary formulas for narrow and self-interested parents and priests. Excessive attention to reason and prudence was even more dangerous to a disinterested morality than excessive indulgence of the passions or sentiments.

Mrs. Radcliffe pressed at the bounds of Rationalism without yielding to Romantic idealism on one hand or to Humean skepticism on the other. She left the door open to feelings she was not willing to indulge herself or to write into her heroine's experiences. The novel of sensibility was, after all, one that pretended (in more or less good faith) to the instruction of its audience—the young ladies most of all—which had to be taught the dangers and limitations of sensibility as well as its prerogatives. The range of Gothic horrors covered during a novel allowed for a full testing of heroine sensibility, but it never left the fair readers in any doubt concerning the ultimate morality and rationality of the world *they* had to deal with. Viciousness was, in the long run, as flimsy as the supernatural extravagances it perpetrated in the imaginings of the heroine. The supernatural in its most lurid forms would probably have flourished without the moral tone with which Mrs. Radcliffe bowdlerized it. But she provided it with a respectable entrée. Once the barriers were so breached, her moral additives to sensationalism were extracted or ignored.

II *Suspense and Expliqué*

Psychological suspense was Mrs. Radcliffe's major contribution to the development of the novel. Before her, novelists like Smollett and, to a lesser extent, Fielding, had made some use of dramatic suspense; but their emphasis is on the action rather than on the passion. In Mrs. Radcliffe, the action is obscured and diminished so that the passion can be intensified through the sensibility and imagination of the character—usually the heroine—on whom the action impinges. Adeline's oft-interrupted reading of the manuscript, Emily's progress to the Marchioness's death chamber, the innumerable prods to psychological fear that fill that chamber, and the dialogues between Schedoni and the Marchesa are full of mental tensions stretched to absolute tautness before exploding in some climactic psychological event which may or may not have an adequate objective correlative in the outside world.

A heroine had only to fulfill the customary stereotype her role called for in the conventional sentimental novel in order to engage the reader in the traumas her imagination created for her. As J. M. S. Tompkins writes, "it was just this sustained command of the reader's nerves that was new." [1] Novels in the Richardsonian tradition, which probed a heroine's emotional distresses, did not have the same grasp on a reader's nerves because the occasions for the lady's distresses were rooted in a psychology of love rather than in fear. And, as Burke indicated, however beautiful love may be, terror exacts a more intense esthetic response in readers vicariously fearing for their lives and mental equilibrium through the mediumship of the same heroine who elsewhere suffers only from love and various kinds of lovers. The additives of terror and the para-supernatural converted the stock heroine into a vehicle for psychological suspense rather than for generalized emotional distress. The world of the domestic sentimental novel was limited and predictable, but, in a world where anything can happen—which is the world of Gothic terrors—suspense is bound to be intensified according to the imaginative capacity of the reader to fill in the dim suggestions of the author with the infinite variety of awful events at his disposal.

Mrs. Radcliffe's happy ingenuity for spinning out suspenseful psychodramas was abetted by rhetorical aids such as the use of contrast and the piling up of dire alternatives. The major contrast was, of course, the exquisite sensibility of the heroine and the illimitable potential for afflicting that sensibility which the villain possessed. The same sensibility, as imagination, compounded the terrors actually afflicting the heroine by intimating to the reader eventualities he would not himself have thought of.

But—again to quote Professor Tompkins—"it is the vice of her method that scenes of raised excitement, where suspense is continually heightened by mystery and unexpected incidents, must be followed by patches of flat explanation." [2] Contemporary critics were not at all in agreement about the virtue or need of the supernatural *expliqués*. In a single issue of the *Monthly Review* (October, 1795) a writer criticizes one Gothic tale because all of the fearful horrors are explicated; another writer states that the principal fault of another work "is that it gives too much encouragement to superstition, by connecting events with preceding predictions, and by visionary appearances, for which the reader is not enabled to account from natural causes." Generally, however, the real criticism of the *expliqué* was that it was trivial: "In like manner we fling back upon the Radcliffe school their . . . ridiculous explanations, and plainly tell them, that they must either confine themselves to ordinary events, or find adequate causes for those horrors and mysteries in which they love to involve us." [3]

Ann Radcliffe's answer to these critics has already been noted or implied. She states again and again that only an overactive imagination in a fear-filled environment (imposed by unnatural agents) could suppose that supernatural agencies were responsible for apparently supernatural phenomena. The very triviality of the *expliqué* emphasized the implicit moral lesson. And, besides, once the emotion has been evoked, it really does not matter whether the cause is real or illusory. Yet later and contemporary critics are likely justified in their wish that Mrs. Radcliffe had exercised her ingenuity less modestly when she explained away her terrors.

III *Influence*

The host of Radcliffean imitators during the 1790's and afterward testifies to her immediate influence, but the deadening sameness of their productions indicates as well the limitations of her art. For writers unable to delay a dénouement through pages of interruptions and suspenseful sidelights on terror, her psychological drama became two-dimensional fast-action with extrinsic incidents piled on one another with little time allowed for a heightened and expansive reaction on the part of a given hero or heroine.

Still, it would be incorrect to ascribe the majority of Gothic novels through 1820 to Mrs. Radcliffe's direct literary influence, though doubtless both their number and their popularity were largely due to her success. She weaned the mass audience of the day from the sentimental and domestic novel to the tale of terror by moralizing her horrors. Her tales therefore received a critical approbation and a generalized reader indulgence that Monk Lewis could not receive. What Lewis could not abide about Radcliffean Gothic—its tedious, sentimental description—was a hallmark of her work. But Lewis's esthetic of sheer terror proved longer lasting; at any rate, the paragraphs full of nature description and various species of sentimental effusions were omitted in the novels of the later horror school.

The critics of the day were certainly aware of Mrs. Radcliffe's faults—the same faults which were sufficient to condemn other authors of the era. They found her descriptions tedious, her *expliqués* contrived, and her characterizations tepid. But they were likewise—sometimes paradoxically—pleased with her rhetoric, with the beauty of certain descriptions, with the happy ingenuity of her patterns of suspense, with her psychological probes—and, of course, with that esthetic *sine qua non*—the unobjectionable moral.

The great writers of the Romantic period were almost all sufficiently influenced by her work to emulate or transcend it. The typically Gothic touches in Wordsworth's *The Borderers* and

"Peter Bell" very likely derive from the more earthbound terrors of her work. The sublime terrors, the "spot of time," in the *Prelude* are Wordsworth's transvaluations of the spiritual suggestions she incorporated into her nature descriptions. Specific portions of his poetry—the "Intimations Ode" most significantly—contain verbal and even philosophical echoes of her work.[4] Coleridge found *Udolpho* the "most interesting" of English novels. His three greatest poems—"Kubla Khan," "The Rime of the Ancient Mariner," and "Christabel"—evidence his own artistic interest in the supernatural. His statement in the *Biographia Literaria*, testifying to his poetic purpose in his portion of the *Lyrical Ballads*, clearly follows Mrs. Radcliffe's practice in her novels of delineating intense human emotions in para-supernatural situations.[5]

Byron's *Manfred* may (in spite of his disclaimer) derive from Goethe's *Faust*, but its Gothic accoutrements suggest a Radcliffean source.[6] Shelley's two sensational Gothic novels are probably inspired by Lewis (or comparable writers), but the mixture of Gothic horror and sentimentality in *The Revolt of Islam* expands his scope to include Mrs. Radcliffe's use of a hero, heroine, and villain to convey a moral lesson. Keats's "The Eve of St. Agnes," "La Belle Dame Sans Merci," and, possibly, "Lamia" illustrate both a general influence and specific verbal remembrances of Ann Radcliffe's work.[7]

Besides the Gothic breed of novelist indiscriminately ascribed to the "Radcliffean School," writers like Scott,[8] Austen,[9] and, later, Dickens[10] and the Brontës,[11] at least tacitly indicate their debt to Mrs. Radcliffe. There were, besides, innumerable translations of her works which made her easily accessible to European writers as romantic as Victor Hugo and as realistic as Honoré de Balzac, both of whom helped to illustrate the fact that her influence on the French was greatest.[12] Her popular appeal at home and abroad was enlarged by the many versions of her novels which appeared with varying success as stage plays. The Gothic allegiance to her work extended through Charles Brockden Brown and Mary Shelley to writers like Bulwer-Lytton and Sheridan Le Fanu. While science fiction predated her influence, the detective story (most immediately in Poe) comprehended some of her terror, much of her shock, a bit of her psychology, a great deal of her suspense, and a more exacting version of her *expliqué*.

There were other writers besides Monk Lewis who profited—

financially at any rate—from Mrs. Radcliffe's example. Theodore Melville, John Palmer, William Ireland, Isabella Kelley, Stephen Cullen, George Walker are a few of the better writers among a host of mediocre imitators of some portion of Mrs. Radcliffe's work. Mary Anne Radcliffe's *Manfroné, or The One-Handed Monk* was often ascribed to Mrs. Radcliffe; it is not a bad imitation, as most ascriptions generally are. With the disappearance of the sensibility heroine, the reader was exposed to the terrors themselves, since the author had no vicarious agency to mediate them.

By the mid-1790's reviewers, as evidenced by a statement in the *Critical Review* of December, 1795, had already become surfeited with run-of-the-mill Gothic novels which lacked not only Radcliffean moral sentiment but also its "wiredrawn" suspense and titillating suggestiveness of horrors always enveloped in obscurity: "The tale of shrieking spectres and bloody murder has been repeated until it palls upon the sense. It requires the genius of a Radcliffe to harrow up our souls with visionary horrors." The six-pence "bluebooks" epitomize the reduction of Radcliffean Gothic to mere shock and fast-action; "It was the aim of the writer of the bluebook to first give his narrative as exciting a title as possible; secondly, to cram into his limited space as many shocking, mysterious, and horrid incidents as possible. Accordingly he must at once rush *in media res* and waste no time in explanation or descriptions, save it be a brief descant on the hero's valour, or his heroine's beauty, or the unknown secrets of the ruined castle." [13]

But Mrs. Radcliffe knew instinctively what later writers who fragmented Gothicism into horror tales and detective stories seldom learned. The story that deals out its action with a series of sledge-hammer blows to the readers' sensibilities finally renders them too callous or too flaccid for a tingling response. We either become impervious or porous to such effects—in any case, unresponsive. By keeping our imaginations on the stretch and our anticipations unbounded, Mrs. Radcliffe lets us aid her in realizing a compendium of potential terrors which collectively elicit and maintain that obscure dread of the unknown which is the major source of the sublime and terrible.

It may be no small praise to have been one of the most influential mediocre writers that English literature has produced, and there is no one with a better claim to that distinction than Ann Radcliffe. The quality of the writers she influenced suggests that such a distinction need not be invidious.

Notes and References

Chapter One

1. Natalie Sarraute, "Rebels in a World of Platitudes," *The Writer's Dilemma* (London, 1961), pp. 37–38.

2. T. N. Talfourd, "Memoir" to *Gaston de Blondeville* (London, 1826). Talfourd is the major source of the biographical information offered here. Other sources are: Clara Frances McIntyre, *Ann Radcliffe in Relation to Her Time* (New Haven, 1920); Alida S. Wieten, *Mrs. Radcliffe—Her Relation Towards Romanticism* (Amsterdam, 1926); Montague Summers, *The Gothic Quest* (London, 1938); Aline Grant, *Ann Radcliffe: A Biography* (Denver, 1951).

3. May 21, 1799. Sir Walter Scott, ed., *Letters of Anna Seward* (London, 1811).

4. The diary excerpts appear in Talfourd's "Memoir."

5. Ann Radcliffe, "On the Supernatural in Poetry," *New Monthly Magazine*, VII (1826), 150.

Chapter Two

1. To Reverend William Cole, March 9, 1765. W. S. Lewis, ed., *The Yale Edition of Horace Walpole's Correspondence*, 30 vols. (New Haven, 1937), I, 88.

2. To Madame du Deffand, March 13, 1767. *Ibid.*, III, 26.

3. Anna Barbauld, ed., *The Old English Baron. A Gothic Story*, vol. xxii, *British Novelists* (London, 1820), p. 5.

4. *Ibid.*

5. See Standley Grean, *Shaftesbury's Philosophy of Religion and Ethics* (Athens, Ohio, 1967), particularly pp. 159–63 and 247–51.

6. Reprints of Economic Classics (New York, 1966), p. 4.

7. Quoted in E. A. Baker, *The History of the English Novel* (New York, 1961), V, 136, fn. (my trans.).

8. Clara Reeve, *The Progress of Romance*, 2 vols. Price et al. (Dublin, 1785). Vol. I, p. 110.

9. O. Elton, ed., "Sentiment and Sensibility in the Eighteenth-Century Novel," *Essays and Studies by Members of the English Association* (Oxford, 1925), pp. 92–93.

10. Boswell's *Life of Johnson,* 2 vols. (London, 1949), I, 427.

11. Letter III to William Cumbe, esq. W. L. Cross, ed. (Oxford, 1927), p. 203.

12. Henry Mackenzie, *The Man of Feeling* (London, 1967), pp. 130–31.

13. Frances Sheridan, *The Memoirs of Miss Sidney Bidulph* (Dublin, 1761), I, 255.

14. Boswell, *op. cit.,* I 241.

15. Quoted by Florence Hilbish, *Charlotte Smith, Poet and Novelist (1749–1806)* (Philadelphia, 1941), p. 137.

16. Charlotte Smith, *Celestina* (London, 1796), IV, 139–40.

17. Anna Barbauld, ed., *British Novelists* (London, 1820), II, 2.

18. Fanny Burney, *Evelina* (London, 1964), p. 37.

19. Fanny Burney, *Cecilia* (London, 1893), II, 173.

20. Fanny Burney, *The Wanderer* (London, 1814), I, 441.

21. Anna Fuller, *The Convent* (London, 1786), I, 15–16.

22. Maria Regina Roche, *The Children of the Abbey* (London, 1843), p. 7.

23. Sophia Lee, *The Recess* (London, 1785), p. 210.

24. A. O. Prickard, trans., *Longinus on the Sublime* (Oxford, 1906), p. 14.

25. Edmund Burke, J. T. Boulton, ed., *A Philosophical Enquiry into the Origin of our Ideas of the Sublime and Beautiful* (New York, 1958), p. 57.

26. *Enquiry,* p. 175.

27. John Dennis, *Miscellanies in Verse and Prose* (London, 1693), pp. 133–34.

28. Hildebrand Jacobs, quoted by Elizabeth Manwaring in *Italian Landscape in Eighteenth Century England: A Study Chiefly of the Influence of Claude Lorrain and Salvator Rosa on English Taste 1700–1800* (London, 1925), p. 20.

29. Quoted in Manwaring, p. 101.

30. *Ibid.,* p. 22.

31. Joseph Warton, *An Essay on the Genius and Writings of Pope,* 2 vols., 4th ed. (London, 1782), II 185.

32. Quoted in Manwaring, p. 177.

33. *Ibid.,* p. 51.

34. *Ibid.,* p. 53.

35. *Ibid.,* p. 149.

36. *Ibid.,* p. 166.

37. *Ibid.,* p. 173.

38. E. S. Barrett, *The Heroine* (London, 1909), p. 35.

39. William Wordsworth, *Guide Through the District of the Lakes* (London, 1951), p. 29.

Chapter Eight

1. J. M. S. Tompkins, *The Popular Novel in England: 1770–1800* (London, 1932), p. 261.

2. *Ibid.*

3. Anon. "Explained Supernatural," *Quarterly Review* (May, 1810).

4. See Frederick L. Beatty ("Mrs. Radcliffe's Fading Gleam," *Philological Quarterly*, January, 1963, 42: 126–29) who demonstrates the great likelihood that Wordsworth was familiar with *The Mysteries of Udolpho* by providing striking verbal and ideological parallels between that novel and the "Intimations Ode."

5. See also D. R. Tuttle ("'Christabel' sources in Percy's *Reliques* and the Gothic Romance," PMLA, June, 1938, 53: 453–66) who provides a compendium of analogous passages between Udolpho and "Christabel." Beatty, in the essay noted above, finds parallels between *Udolpho* and Coleridge's "Mad Monk" which suggest that either the latter poem and the "Intimations Ode" had a cognate source in *Udolpho* or that Coleridge's reading of *Udolpho* filtered through the "Mad Monk" to influence Wordsworth.

6. See also M. L. Farrand ("*The Mysteries of Udolpho and Childe Harold*," MLN, April, 1930, 45: 220–21) who finds parallels between Emily St. Aubert's first view of Venice and stanzas 1, 2, and 18 of Canto IV of *Childe Harold*.

7. M. H. Shackford ("The Eve of St. Agnes and *The Mysteries of Udolpho*," January, 1921, 36:104–18) finds many verbal echoes between the works she takes up, but Amy Lowell (*John Keats*, II, 161–65, Boston, 1925) calls most of them into question, without, however, denying that the pervasive influence of Mrs. Radcliffe's works could well have permeated Keats's imagination to find its way into his work.

8. Scott's introductory comments on Mrs. Radcliffe in his Ballantyne edition of her works effectively qualify whatever disparagement his early disclaimers of imitating Mrs. Radcliffe might have contained. Novels like *The Monastery*, *The Black Dwarf*, and *The Bride of Lammermoor* certainly leave him open to a strong suspicion of any influence he tended to discount for what were doubtless good practical as well as esthetic reasons. Mrs. Radcliffe was becoming passé.

9. *Northanger Abbey*'s complimentary satire of *The Mysteries of Udolpho* and *The Romance of the Forest*, written at the height of the Gothic fad (1798), demonstrates that, like Henry Tilney, Jane Austen could appreciate the relative superiority of Mrs. Radcliffe's works and discriminate them (as perhaps Catherine Morland could not) not only from life but also from flatwork pieces like *Horrid Mysteries* and the run-of-the-mill variety of domestic and translated "German" shockers.

10. Mrs. Haversham and her chamber in *Great Expectations* offer a classic example.

11. Particularly the hero-villains of *Wuthering Heights* and *Jane Eyre*, who began in Montoni and were filtered through the Byronic hero.

12. Reviewing his own work in 1832, Balzac's genial egoism overflows from self-appreciation to a comment on the "admirable novels of Mrs. Radcliffe" and specific "popularity of *The Mysteries of Udolpho*." (Quoted by Frederick Lawton in *Balzac*, London, 1910.)

13. Montague Summers, *The Gothic Quest* (London, 1938), p. 83.

Selected Bibliography

PRIMARY SOURCES

A Journey made in the summer of 1794, through Holland and the Western Frontiers of Germany, with a return down the Rhine, to which are added Observations during a tour to the Lakes of Lancashire, Westmoreland and Cumberland. London: G. G. and J. Robinson, 1795.
The Novels of Ann Radcliffe. London: John Ballantyne, 1821.
T. N. Talfourd, "Memoir" in *Gaston de Blondeville.* London: H. Colburn, 1826.

SECONDARY SOURCES

BAKER, E. A. *The History of the English Novel.* Vol. V. New York: Barnes and Noble, Inc., 1961. Contains a clear, succinct account of the major Gothic writers.
BIRKHEAD, EDITH. "Sentiment and Sensibility in the Eighteenth-Century Novel." *Essays and Studies by Members of the English Association.* Oxford: Clarendon Press, 1925. A good short study of an important eighteenth-century distinction.
GRANT, ALINE. *Ann Radcliffe: A Biography.* Denver: Alan Swallow, 1951. Popular biography which, however, contains some new material.
MANWARING, ELIZABETH. *Italian Landscape in Eighteenth Century England: A Study chiefly of the Influence of Claude Lorrain and Salvator Rosa on English Taste 1700–1800.* London: Frank Cass & Co. Ltd., 1925. Indispensable for an understanding of the interest in landscape art which justified Mrs. Radcliffe's lengthy descriptive passages.
McINTRYE, CLARA FRANCES. *Ann Radcliffe in Relation to Her Time.* New Haven: Yale University Press, 1920. Emphasizes Mrs. Radcliffe's significance in developing the principle of suspense in the novel.
PRAZ, MARIO. *The Romantic Agony.* London: Oxford University Press,

1933. Contains psychological (and psychosexual) accounts of the Gothic novel.

RAILO, EINO. *The Haunted Castle*. London: G. Rutledge & Sons, 1927. Exhaustive study of the various themes and motives in the Gothic novel.

SUMMERS, MONTAGUE. *A Gothic Bibliography*. London: Fortune Press, 1940. Most comprehensive listing of Gothic novels.

————. *The Gothic Quest*. London: Fortune Press, 1938. Includes a detailed account of Monk Lewis and many lesser Gothic writers. Critical comment less helpful.

TOMPKINS, J. M. S. *The Popular Novel in England: 1770–1800*. London: Constable & Co., 1932. Contains excellent chapter on the Gothic Romance.

VARMA, DEVENDRA P. *The Gothic Flame*. New York: Russell & Russell, 1957. Most recent full-length study of the Gothic novel emphasizes the metaphysical and surrealistic overtones of the genre.

WARE, MALCOLM. *Sublimity in the Novels of Ann Radcliffe*. Copenhagen: Lundequistska Bokhandln, 1963. Comprehensive selection of passages in Mrs. Radcliffe's work which illustrates Burke's analysis of the sublime, but restriction to Burke's theory is too exclusive.

WIETEN, ALIDA S. *Mrs. Radcliffe—Her Relation Towards Romanticism*. Amsterdam: H. J. Paris, 1926. Emphasizes the poetry; shows direct influence on Romantic writers.

Index

Addison, Joseph, 54; *The Spectator,* 30; *The Guardian,* 30
Arabian Nights, 30
Aristotle, 29
Arnaud, Baculard d', 35-36, 38
Austen, Jane, 45, 165; *Northanger Abbey,* 19, 48; *Pride and Prejudice,* 82

Baillie, Joanna, *Plays on the Passions,* 18
Balzac, Honoré de, 165
Barrett, E. S., *The Heroine,* 47, 59
Beckford, William, *Vathek,* 31
Behn, Aphra, 18
Berkeley, George, 160
Birkhead, Edith, "Sentiment and Sensibility in the Eighteenth Century Novel," 41
Blair, Robert, "The Grave," 30
Boileau, Nicolas, 51
Book of Job, 29
Brontë, Charlotte and Emily Jane, 165
Brown, Charles Brockden, 165
Brown, Lancelot ("Capability"), 56, 57
Bulwer-Lytton, Edward, 165
Burke, Edmund, 16 20-21, 51, 54, 57, 147, 162; on landscape 55, 59; *Enquiry into the Origin of our Ideas of the Sublime and Beautiful,* 20, 49-50, 53; on esthetic of terror, 60
Burney, Fanny, *Evelina,* 45; *The Wanderer,* 45, 46; *Cecilia,* 45

Byron, George Gordon (Lord), *Manfred,* 165

Carter, Elizabeth, 17-18, 58
Chatterton, Thomas, 36; Bishop Rowley Poems, 37
Chaucer, Geoffrey, 29
Coleridge, Samuel Taylor, 35, 69; "The Rime of the Ancient Mariner," 39, 165; *Biographia Literaria,* 39, 165; "Kubla Khan," 165; "Christabel," 165; *Lyrical Ballads,* 165
Collins, William, 15, 161
Constable, John, 58
Critical Review, The, 56, 166
Cullen, Stephen, 166

Dante (Alighieri), 29
Dennis, John, 54
Dickens, Charles, 43, 165
Dyer, John, "The Fleece," 56

English Chronicle, 16

Fielding, Henry, 19, 162; *Tom Jones,* 40, 82
Fox, Charles, 19
Fuller, Anne, *The Convent,* or *The History of Sophia Nelson,* 46, 47, 48

Goethe, Johann Wolfgang von, *Faust,* 165
Goldsmith, Oliver, *The Citizen of the World,* 30

Gothic devices: 14, 38, 56; in Radcliffe, 13, 27, 29, 75, 78, 83, 98, 103-4, 152; in Walpole, 13, 32; in Smollett, 29-30; in Graveyard poets, 30; in Arnaud, 35-36

Gothicism, French, 35; English, 29, 35, 36; German, 35; Elizabethan, 29; Jacobean, 29; Oriental, 30; Radcliffean, 13, 14, 33, 34, 37, 41, 71, 166-67; Walpolean, 13, 14; features of, 90; adventures in, 125; see also Gothic devices

"Graveyard" poets, 30, 31, 34, 58

Gray, Thomas, 15, 161

Green, Thomas, 57

Hartley, David, 37

Hawkins, Sir John, 55

Hero, see Radcliffe Ann

Herodotus, 29

Heroic Romance, French, 47

Heroine, Austen, 82; Fielding, 82; Richardson, 82; Shakespeare, 64-65; Sentimental, 19, 46, 79, 87; see also Radcliffe, Ann

Homer, 98

Hugo, Victor, 138

Hume, David, 37

Hurd, Richard (Bishop), Letters on Chivalry and Romance, 36

Hutcheson, Francis, 37

Ireland, William, 166

Johnson, Samuel, 16, 37, 40, 41, 44, 55, 118, 134; Rasselas, 30

Keate, George, 56

Keats, John, 51; "Grecian Urn," 161; "The Eve of St. Agnes," 165; "La Belle Dame Sans Merci," 165; "Lamia," 165

Kelley, Isabella, 166

Knight, Richard Payne, 56

LaFayette, Madame de, The Princess of Cleves, 40

Lee, Sophia, The Recess, 15, 34, 49-50

Le Fanu, Sheridan, 165

Leland, Thomas, 75; Longsword, 40

Lewis, Matthew ("Monk"), 60, 72, 85, 164, 165; The Monk, 19, 139

Locke, John, 109

Longinus, On the Sublime, 51

Lorrain, Claude, 16, 24, 55, 56, 57, 58, 59, 132

Mackenzie, Henry, The Man of Feeling, 43

Macpherson, James, 36; Ossian, 16, 37

Mallet, David, "Excursion," 30

Maturin, Charles, 72, 85

Melville, Theodore, 166

Milton, John, 21, 36, 39, 87; Il Penseroso, 30; Paradise Lost, 142; Comus, 142; Areopagitica, 142

Minerva Press, 35

Montagu, Elizabeth, 57

Odysseus, 29

Oriental tale, 30, 31

Palmer, John, 166

Parnell, Thomas, "Night Piece on Death," 30

Peacock, Thomas Love, 22

Percy, Thomas, Reliques of Ancient English Poetry, 35

Picturesque, 55-57. See also Lorrain, Claude; Poussin, Nicolas; Radcliffe, Ann; Rosa, Salvator

Poe, Edgar Allen, 165

Poussin, Nicolas, 55, 56, 115

Prévost, Antoine (Abbé), 35, 41; Life of Cleveland, 40

Price, Uvedale, 56, 59

Radcliffe, Ann (Ward), action, 89, 135; catholicism, 24, 75, 85, 138-39, 158; disinterestedness, 64, 66, 80, 103, 106-8, 119, 133, 160; decor, 25-26, 84, 90, 94-96, 112, 155-56; drama, 74, 88-89, 98, 103, 107, 124; ethic, 64, 80, 160; expliqué, 17, 18, 70, 109-10, 111, 114-15, 119, 122, 125, 126, 129,

8 7 3 9 7

131-32, 134, 158, 159-64; gothic features, 84, 90, 125, 148; hero, 48, 70, 135, 145-49, 155-58; heroine, 28, 50, 55, 57, 58, 64, 66, 67, 70, 75, 79-84, 87, 93, 95, 99-104, 112, 130, 134, 149-55, 162-64; horror, 52, 55, 67, 73-74, 84, 85, 90, 93-94, 99, 102-3, 128-29, 154, 162; humor, 109; influence, 164-67; moral dilemma, 13, 68, 133; misleading, 129-30, 147; morality, 16, 18, 19, 27, 28, 63, 64, 87, 103, 106, 109, 115, 127, 128-33, 141, 144, 159, 161; parental authority, 89, 137-38; picturesque, 13, 21-27, 37, 57-58, 76, 88, 94, 112, 113, 117, 119, 127, 132, 148-51, 160, 164; religious authority, 137-38; sensibility, 17, 64, 66, 80, 83, 93-94, 97, 102, 117, 119, 123, 127-28, 130, 159-63; sentimentality, 24, 25, 61, 108, 115-19, 149; style, 70-74, 88, 97-99, 109, 111, 121, 151; supernatural, 110, 125-27, 134, 147, 158, 162-64; surprise 121; suspense, 73, 75, 79, 97-98, 141, 149; terror, 37, 82, 88, 91, 108, 125, 127, 152-53; villain, 68-70, 75, 79-82, 100, 104-9, 135, 137-44, 145-49, 154-55; villainess, 75, 137-44; and Walpole, 13, 61, 70, 112; *see also* Gothic devices, Gothicism
WRITINGS OF:
The Castles of Athlin and Dunbayne, 15, 61-74, 110, 151; *Gaston de Blondeville,* 15, 20, 25, 27; *Journey through Holland Etc. Made in the Summer of 1794,* 19-20, 21, 22, 24, 25; *The Italian,* 19, 20, 75, 134-58; *The Mysteries of Udolpho,* 13, 16, 19, 20, 21, 22, 24, 26, 34, 54, 93, 110, 112-34; *The Romance of the Forest,* 19, 22, 25, 34, 58, 90-111, 125, 144, 152, 157; *The Sicilian Romance,* 25, 75-89, 110, 144
Radcliffe, Mary Ann, *Manfroné,* 166
Radcliffe, William, 16, 19

Reeve, Clara, 40, 41, 43; *The Old English Baron,* 32, 33, 36, 39; *The Champion of Virtue—A Gothic Story,* 33, 34; *Progress of Romance,* 39, 40
Richardson, Samuel, 19, 75; *Clarissa,* 35, 41, 42, 44, 82; *Pamela,* 40
Roche, Maria Regina, *The Children of the Abbey,* 47
Rosa, Salvator, 16, 23, 55, 56, 57, 58, 59, 66, 115
Rousseau, Jean-Jacques, 35

Sade, Donatien, Marquis de, *Justine,* 19
Schiller, Johann, *The Robbers* (Die Räuber), 15, 35
Scott, Sir Walter, 17, 54, 165
Sensibility, Gothic, 36, 37, 45; moral, 37; Sternesque, 47; Mackenzian, 47. *See also* Radcliffe, Ann
Seward, Anna, 18, 57
Shaftesbury, Anthony Ashley Cooper (3rd Earl of), 37, 55
Shakespeare, William, 21, 29, 31, 36, 37, 51, 54, 65; *Hamlet,* 26, 49, 121, 126, 147-48; *Romeo and Juliet,* 109; *Measure for Measure,* 64; *Macbeth,* 141; Othello, 67-68, 139
Shelley, Mary, 72, 165
Shelley, Percy Bysshe, *The Revolt of Islam,* 165
Sheridan, Frances, 44; *The Memoirs of Miss Sidney Bidulph,* 43
Sheridan, Richard, 19
Smith, Adam, *Treatise on Moral Sentiments,* 38
Smith, Charlotte, 44; *The Old Manor House,* 34, 44; *Celestina,* 44
Smollet, Tobias George, 19, 40, 45; *Ferdinand Count Fathom,* 29-30
Sophocles, 29
Spenser, Edmund, 36, 39
Sterne, Laurence, 19, 41, 42; *The Sentimental Journey,* 42
Sublime, 52-53, 59. *See also* Burke, Edmund

Summers, Montague, 16
Swift, Jonathan, *Gulliver's Travels,* 30

Talfourd, T. N., "Memoir" to Ann Radcliffe's *Gaston de Blondeville,* 15, 16, 17, 19, 21, 26-27
Thomson, James, 15; *The Seasons,* 56
Tompkins, J.M.S., 162, 163
Tourneur, Cyril, 29

Verdi, Giuseppe, *Rigoletto,* 138

Walker, George, 166
Walpole, Horace, 32-33, 39, 42, 60, 61, 70, 72, 75, 112; *The Castle of Otranto,* 13, 29, 33. *See also* Gothic devices, Gothicism
Warton, Joseph, 19, 36, 56-57
Warton, Thomas, 36
Webster, John, 29
Wedgwood, Josiah, 15
Wordsworth, William, 42, 60, 160; "Tintern Abbey," 160-61; *The Prelude,* 23, 165; *The Guide to the Lakes,* 59; *The Borderers,* 164-65; "Peter Bell," 164-65; "Intimations Ode," 165

Young, Edward, "Night Thoughts on Life, Death and Immortality," 30, 35, 36

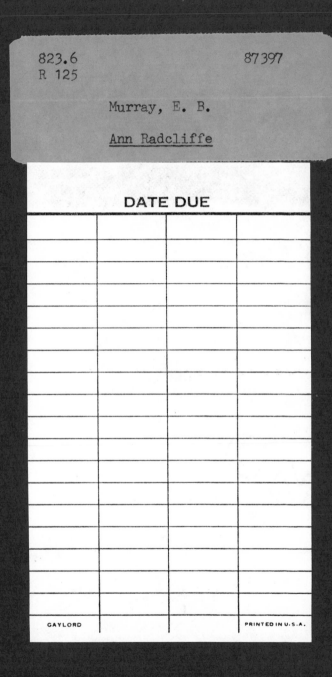

DATE DUE

GAYLORD			PRINTED IN U.S.A.